Negaholic®
No
More!

By
Dr. Chérie Carter-Scott

National Press Publications

A Division of Rockhurst University Continuing Education Center, Inc.
6901 West 63rd St., P.O. Box 2949, Shawnee Mission, KS 66201-1349
1-800-258-7248 • 1-913-432-7757

National Seminars endorses nonsexist language. However, in an effort to make this Business User's Manual clear, consistent and easy to read, we've used the generic "he" throughout and generic "she" throughout. The copy is not intended to be sexist.

About Rockhurst University
Continuing Education Center, Inc.

Rockhurst University Continuing Education Center, Inc., is committed to providing lifelong learning opportunities through the integration of innovative education and training.

National Seminars Group, a division of Rockhurst University Continuing Education Center, Inc., has its finger on the pulse of America's business community. We've trained more than 2 million people in every imaginable occupation to be more productive and advance their careers. Along the way, we've learned a few things. What it takes to be successful ... how to build the skills to make it happen ... and how to translate learning into results. Millions of people from thousands of companies around the world turn to National Seminars for training solutions.

National Press Publications is our product and publishing division. We offer a complete line of the finest self-study and continuous-learning resources available anywhere. These products present our industry-acclaimed curriculum and training expertise in a concise, action-oriented format you can put to work right away. Packed with real-world strategies and hands-on techniques, these resources are guaranteed to help you meet the career and personal challenges you face every day.

Legend Symbol Guide

Exercises that reinforce your learning experience

Questions that will help you apply the critical points to your situation

Checklists that will help you identify important issues for future application

Key issues to learn and understand for future application

C
A
S
E

S
T
U
D
Y

Real-world case studies that will help you apply the information you've learned

Table of Contents

INTRODUCTION

More than 25 years ago, I began studying Negativity and its effect on people, especially in the workplace. (In fact, I feel so strongly about how it impacts peoples' lives that I always capitalize the word. You'll see it written this way throughout the book.) I even created the term Negaholic® to describe someone who is deeply embedded in his or her own Negativity.

So just where does this Negativity come from? It typically grows out of the change we seem to encounter in our daily lives. Humans, by nature, are creatures of habit. For the most part, we like doing the same things in the same way with the same people. But once in awhile life throws us a curve ball, and we have to scramble to get out of the way. In other words, we have to make a change.

And when change keeps us from achieving our goals or doing what we want to do, Negativity can set in. If we allow it to grow and fester, then we've got a case of Negaholism on our hands. People don't like to admit they're Negaholics — they often try to hide it. Unfortunately, this never works. If you deny it exists or try to use positive thinking as a Band-Aid, the symptoms will only worsen and eventually cripple you and those around you.

Negativity needs to be addressed and dealt with. It certainly won't go away on its own. That's where this book can help. It provides tools, techniques and exercises to help you overcome Negaholism, adapt to change and lead a healthy and happy life. In particular, it discusses how change and stress affect Negativity, what makes people Negative, how Negativity spreads throughout organizations and, finally, what you can do about your own Negativity.

Getting started is often the hardest part. Just by picking up this book you've made a positive first step. Good luck and good reading.

*C*HAPTER 1

Are You a Negaholic?

Let's begin with some self-reflection. Do any of the following situations sound a little too familiar?

- Do you ever talk yourself out of trying something new — such as skiing or country-line dancing — because you don't want to look stupid?
- Do you ever talk yourself out of a relationship because you think the other person is out of your league (too attractive, too outgoing, too successful)?
- Do you ever tell yourself you can't enter an athletic competition because you've never done it before or because you're afraid of failure?
- Do you ever tell yourself you can't lose weight because you don't have any willpower or you just like to eat too much?
- Do you ever talk yourself out of buying something you really want — such as a stylish new dress or a fine antique table — because you don't trust your own tastes and you don't think others will like it?
- Do you ever avoid buying the car you really want because you're afraid it's too flashy, too impractical and too expensive?

- Do you ever talk yourself out of a job opportunity because you're afraid you might not measure up?
- Do you ever give up on planning a great vacation because you know some crisis will erupt at work and force you to cancel your plans?
- Do you ever dread going to the office because you have to face your co-workers and deal with the internal politics for yet another day?
- Do you ever avoid certain co-workers so you don't have to interact with them at all or only when it's absolutely necessary?
- Do you ever get tired of the inconsistencies at work and feel that your organization's direction, strategies, policies and procedures change from day to day?
- Do you ever find it frustrating that certain philosophies and attitudes are supported verbally but not put into practice?
- Do you ever find yourself longing for retirement and feeling as if you're simply biding your time?

If you answered "yes" to any of these questions, then you probably have some Negaholic tendencies. They may affect your personal life or professional life or both. (Later in this chapter, you'll take a test to determine if you're truly a Negaholic.)

What Is a Negaholic?

To understand the meaning of the term, let's break it down into two parts:

1. Nega = negative
2. Holic = a person who's addicted to something

Very simply stated, a Negoholic is a person who's addicted to Negativity. The word Negativity comes from the Latin root "negare," which means "to deny." And when you deny something, you're saying you can't do it. You can't try something new; you can't lose weight; you can't accept a challenging job assignment; you can't deal with your co-workers.

These "I can'ts" take over your life. You have trouble saying "I can" and believing that you're capable, competent, lovable and deserving of what you really want. It's as if there's an intense inner-war being waged, with the "I can'ts" overpowering the "I cans." You become trapped in a private prison emblazoned with graffiti that says: "You can't be it. You can't do it. You can't have it. So forget it!"

This Negativity may be housed deep inside your own private prison, but it's impossible to keep it a secret. It's reflected in your attitudes, thoughts, words and actions. For example, Negaholic children learn very early on that they'll receive more attention for being sick, getting hurt, having a messy room, causing trouble, telling lies and, in general, being difficult. In other words, their motivation comes from Negative behavior rather than positive behavior. They become addicted to the psychological "rush" associated with dwelling on Negative attitudes, thoughts, words and actions.

The "I Can/I Can't" Game

You've heard of mind games. Well, one of the mind's favorites is the "I can/I can't" game. It causes you to be positive and self-confident one minute and Negative and self-doubting the next.

Here's an example. Have you ever been in an audience listening to a presenter do his "shtick" and secretly thought to yourself, "I could do that. Why, I could even do it better — maybe 10 times better"? This is the "I can" side of you coming out. This side wants you to toot your own horn and show your stuff. This side believes you can meet any

"To do nothing is the way to be nothing."

Nathaniel Howe

3

challenge and live your life exactly as you want. This side of you is capable, confident, self-sufficient, fearless and almost always certain about everything. It is never confused or crippled by doubt.

But the "I can" side can quickly vanish. Say your boss asks you to make a presentation in front of dozens of sales representatives gathered for an annual meeting. Although you're flattered by the request, you begin to doubt your experience, your expertise and ability to do it. A little voice inside tells you: "You can't do that! You've never done anything like that before. You don't know what you're doing, and everyone will realize it the minute you open your mouth. If you don't say no, you're going to look like a fool." And suddenly, the "I can" side that was so sure you could give a great presentation is having second thoughts.

If you've ever heard voices like these, then you know all about the "I can't" side. These voices come out to protect you and keep you from making a fool of yourself and from being embarrassed or humiliated. They also keep you from taking risks and doing anything that pushes you beyond your comfort zone. Ultimately, the voices keep you timid, hesitant and full of self-doubt and fear.

I refer to this part of you as the "I can't self." One of the biggest challenges in life is learning how to break away from the "I can't self" — to conquer the "I can'ts." It's a learning process that takes time.

These two sides are always clashing and jockeying for position inside of you. It seems just when you're about to stretch outside your comfort zone, go for a big goal or take a big risk (the "I can" side), the "I can't" side shows itself. It tries to dissuade and distract you, get you to play it safe, and protect you from disappointment and failure. It works on the premise that if you don't risk too much, then you won't fall as far if you fail. And, of course, the odds are that you will fail.

Care to guess who wins almost all of these contests? Easy, it's the "I can't self." A big bully like this doesn't have a chance against the "I can" weakling.

The real problem is that the "I can't self" gets carried away and becomes more than protective — it becomes downright critical. It criticizes your wants, telling you that you're wrong to want them, they're beyond your grasp and you're wasting your time. So, why try for them in the first place?

If you leave your "I can't self" unchecked, it will take over your life. It will dictate who you are, what you can do and what you have and don't have. In reality, it will severely limit your life in order to keep you safe and protected.

The "Negattack"

When the "I can'ts" seize you and take over your life, you're suffering from a "Negattack." A "Negattack" runs roughshod over all your hopes, dreams and ambitions. Like a band of outlaws, a "Negattack" ravages and plunders, showing no concern for your feelings. Unfortunately, your "I can self" isn't strong enough to form a posse and try to head the "Negattack" off at the pass. Instead, your "I can self" sits quietly and passively and therefore gets trampled every time the "I can't" gang rides into town.

If you've ever been the victim of a "Negattack" or you find yourself saying "I can't" more often than you'd like, then you may be a Negaholic or at least have Negaholic tendencies. To find out for sure, spend a few minutes completing The Negaholic Self-Assessment Tool that follows. It will help you determine to what degree you're a Negaholic and just how serious your condition is.

The first steps in confronting any problem are knowing and admitting that you have a problem. The Negaholic Self-Assessment Tool will assist you in accomplishing these two steps. If you are a Negaholic, the remainder of this Business User's Manual will allow you to know yourself better, better

> *"The setting of a great hope is like the setting of the sun. The brightness of our life is gone."*
>
> Henry Wadsworth Longfellow

understand your behavior patterns and, most importantly, change your old habits so you can have a happier and healthier relationship with yourself.

The Negaholic Self-Assessment Tool

For each of the following 50 questions, please circle yes or no.

YES NO 1. Do you sometimes have difficulty getting out of bed in the morning?

YES NO 2. Do you sometimes focus on all the times when you "blew it" and things didn't work out?

YES NO 3. Do you often find yourself expecting the worst so as not to be disappointed?

YES NO 4. Do you sometimes observe yourself feeling anxious when you hear good news in anticipation of the bad that will surely follow?

YES NO 5. When asked "What do you want?" do you frequently answer "I don't know."

YES NO 6. Do you often hear yourself saying "It doesn't matter" when you are asked what you want?

YES NO 7. Do you often find yourself citing the mistakes, blunders, mishaps and boo-boos in your past as justification not to take another risk?

YES NO 8. When imaging a "big goal," do you hear the voices in your head saying "You can't do that!" or "You'll never be able to ...!"?

YES NO 9. Do you have difficulty being enthusiastic about your "to do" list?

YES NO 10. Do you frequently find fault with little things you do?

YES NO 11. Do you hear yourself putting yourself down regarding what you wear, how you walk, what you say?

YES NO 12. Do you have lists of things you have never accomplished that you use against yourself?

YES NO 13. Do you have difficulty celebrating your accomplishments?

YES NO 14. When you start to imagine your goals, do you hear "Who do you think you are?" in your head?

YES NO 15. When friends compliment you, do you brush it off, dismiss it or look for an ulterior motive?

YES NO 16. When you look in the mirror do you often count the gray hairs and wrinkles?

Do you think you could ever …

YES NO 17. Have the dream home you want?

YES NO 18. Have the ideal relationship that you want?

YES NO 19. Make the amount of money that you want?

YES NO 20. Have the body you want?

YES NO 21. Have a job that you enjoy, which is satisfying and rewarding?

Do you frequently get angry at yourself …

YES NO 22. For spending too much or being a cheapskate?

YES NO 23. For eating too much?

YES NO 24. For drinking too much?

YES NO 25. For wasting time?

Do you frequently feel …

YES NO 26. Angry at yourself or others?

YES NO 27. Anxious in general or in specific?

YES NO 28. Confused about what to do?

YES NO 29. Depressed about anything or nothing?

YES NO 30. Hesitant?

YES   NO   31. Impatient?
YES   NO   32. Insecure?
YES   NO   33. Lonely?
YES   NO   34. Regretful?
YES   NO   35. Unhappy?
YES   NO   36. Unloved?
YES   NO   37. Worried?

Do you seldom feel ...
YES   NO   38. Calm?
YES   NO   39. Capable?
YES   NO   40. Certain?
YES   NO   41. Competent?
YES   NO   42. Confident?
YES   NO   43. Enthusiastic?
YES   NO   44. Happy?
YES   NO   45. Joyful?
YES   NO   46. Lovable?
YES   NO   47. Optimistic?
YES   NO   48. Powerful?
YES   NO   49. Satisfied?
YES   NO   50. Do you constantly work and strive but rarely experience completion and satisfaction?

Scoring:
- Give yourself 2 points for every YES answer for questions 1-15.
- Give yourself 2 points for every NO answer for questions 16-21.
- Give yourself 2 points for every YES answer for questions 22-50.
- Total your points and find yourself on the scale below.

   0   Congratulations! You have an excellent self-image, high self-esteem and a happy, healthy and full life.

1-24 You have a mild case of Negaholism and very little to worry about. With some affirmations, positive reinforcement and pats on the back from yourself and your loved ones, you'll be just fine.

25-40 You definitely have Negaholic tendencies, which probably run in your family. If you address your condition now, you can recover. Left untreated, however, it could grow into something extremely bad for your mental health. Consider seeking out a consciousness-raising group, a self-esteem workshop, a self-help group or therapy. Also read books about building a positive self-image a few times each year.

41-60 You need to take your condition seriously. Without proper care and attention, you will become a full-blown Negaholic. You need some form of positive imaging every week in order to turn this condition around. Try keeping a journal of your feelings, reading self-help books and listening to self-help audiotapes in the car or before you go to sleep each night.

61-80 You're in the danger zone. No longer should you cover your condition up, try to take things in stride or hope everything will correct itself when you lose that weight, meet the right person or get the right job. It's time to face the fact that you're seriously addicted to Negativity. Emotionally, you're beating yourself to death. There is hope, however. You are not a lost cause. The first step is to

acknowledge that you're a Negaholic, and then second is to commit to doing something about it, such as the suggestions previously mentioned.

81-100 You're a confirmed Negaholic. Admit it and immediately begin taking steps to deal with your addiction each day. At this point, it has become bigger than you are. In fact, your Negativity is so subtle that you hardly notice it, yet it pervades your every thought and feeling. Now is a critical time to detoxify the demon living within you. Start by reading this book and following the steps it outlines. Don't wait another day. A new life and a positive self-image can be yours!

Questions for Personal Development

1. What is the major emphasis of this chapter?

   _____

   _____

   _____

2. What are the most important things you learned from this chapter?

   _____

   _____

   _____

3. How can you apply what you learned to your current job?

   _____

   _____

   _____

4. How will you go about making these changes?

_____

_____

_____

5. How can you monitor improvement?

_____

_____

_____

6. Summarize the changes you expect to see in yourself one year from now.

_____

_____

_____

C *HAPTER 2*

Different Types of Negaholics

Now that you've taken and scored the Negaholic Self-Assessment Tool, you should know your current condition. You should understand how much Negativity impacts your life. At this point, you probably find yourself in one of three places:

1. On the bridge. You're so mired in your Negativity that you think you're beyond help. You're ready to quietly end it all. Whatever you do, don't jump! There's always hope!

2. On the fence. You're worried about your condition and you're also uncertain if you can be helped. You feel up to facing your Negativity, but what if you're a hopeless case?

3. On the road to recovery. You're excited that someone has written a book for Negaholics, and you're ready to race toward a cure.

Whichever stage you find yourself, you need to learn as much as possible about Negaholism. Simply stated, Negaholism is a deep feeling of insufficiency. You feel that you just don't measure up — whether it's on the job or at home. For example, you may believe it's useless to apply for that promotion at work because you're just not qualified or competent enough. Or you may have given

> *"Life is made up of sobs, sniffles, and smiles, with sniffles predominating."*
>
> O. Henry

up trying to find a soul mate because you're just not outgoing or attractive enough.

If you become consumed by these feelings of insufficiency, then you're a Negaholic. And Negaholics are addicts just like people who depend on alcohol or drugs. Here's one way to think about it:

> ***All addictions are the result of the pursuit of or the avoidance of a feeling!***

Take alcoholics and drug addicts. They drink or take drugs to get high (pursuing a feeling) so they don't have to face the bad things in their lives (avoiding a feeling). In the same way, Negaholics continually tell themselves they can't do something (pursuing a feeling) so they won't have to face possible failure (avoiding a feeling).

Four Categories of Negaholics

During the past 25 years, I've met all kinds of Negaholics. Although they have different forms of the disease, they typically demonstrate their negative attitudes and feelings through words and actions. To keep things simple, I've divided Negaholics into four major categories:

1. **Attitudinal Negaholics** are successful people who drive themselves relentlessly. To those on the outside, they appear calm, orderly, neat and attractive — in other words, they're on top of everything and seemingly have it all together. In reality, this couldn't be farther from the truth. On the inside, they're tormented and never satisfied. Because they hide their true feelings so well, the people in this group suffer from the most subtle form of Negaholism.

2. **Behavioral Negaholics** may succeed in spite of themselves, but they usually miss the mark due to self-sabotage. Because they try so hard, you don't

want to find fault with them. While they realize there's a discrepancy between their ideas and their actions, they can't seem to break away from their well-established behavior patterns. Behavioral Negaholics tend to over-do, whether it's too much smoking, eating, drinking, drug abuse, sex, gambling, exercising or watching TV.

3. **Mental Negaholics** are constantly flogging themselves for something. Once they latch on to something they've said or done, they can't let it go — they're relentless about it. They intently focus on the past, the present and the future by offering criticism, judgments and mental abuse.

4. **Verbal Negaholics** are hopeless, helpless and resistant to change. They constantly say Negative things about themselves, other people, places and situations. The amazing thing is they don't have the slightest idea they're being Negative. Instead, they believe they're accurately reporting the facts — as they see them, of course.

Just as there are different types of Negaholics, there are different degrees of Negaholism. In its mildest form, Negaholism gives victims a reasonable amount of awareness of their disease. They usually acknowledge they need help and sometimes seek it out. With moderate forms of Negaholism, victims have only a limited awareness of their addiction, which makes treatment a little more difficult. In the most extreme form, Negaholism is a chronic condition. The "I can'ts" have completely taken over and are totally in charge. The chances for a cure are slimmest.

2

Attitudinal Negaholism

Now let's more closely examine each type of Negaholic.

People who suffer from Attitudinal Negaholism, are never satisfied. Deep down they believe that it's impossible to truly enjoy life. In the game of life, they always lose and never win. When they set standards or goals for themselves, they make them impossible to attain. They can never be good enough, do enough or have enough to satisfy the relentless inner-demon that drives them. Some specific examples are "The Perfectionist," "The Never Good Enough" and "The Slave Driver."

"The Perfectionist"

"The Perfectionist" is a good news/bad news sort. He always sets high standards — some might consider them unreasonable standards — and any that fall short are just unacceptable. He expects perfection from himself and from everyone around him. Imperfection is not tolerated.

So what's the good news? You'll always get the most and the best from "The Perfectionist." That's a plus if he works for you. The bad news is that it's difficult, if not impossible, to please him. That's a negative if you work for him. Eventually you'll get the ax because you can't possibly measure up to his standards on an ongoing basis. In many cases, he'll resort to doing things himself rather than delegating them to incompetents.

The pressure to perform to "The Perfectionist's" standards is just too intense. Since there are few, if any, people who fill the bill of perfection, "The Perfectionist" ends up feeling self-righteous and better than everyone else. Ultimately, he also feels lonely.

You may wonder how "The Perfectionist" can be a Negaholic. However, if you take a psychological drill and go deep enough into his attitude, you almost always discover a deep-seated fear of not being good enough, of being inadequate.

"Trifles make perfection, and perfection is no trifle."

Michelangelo

Profile of "The Perfectionist"

I met Dwayne, a fit, well-dressed, "not a hair out of place" business executive, when he came for an office visit. His warm, inviting smile and firm handshake conveyed self-confidence and control. His demeanor seemed almost too rehearsed.

He began, "I don't know why I'm here, but Robin, my fiancee, said that you were good to talk to about transitions and career changes. I know what I want, and I strategize and plan so that I get what I want."

I asked him what transition or career change he was encountering.

"Well, I'm currently in the computer business, but it's time to make a change. Now I want to go into the telecommunications business," he said in a strange way.

Of course, I inquired why he wanted out of computers.

"I've had it with computers, and I've learned all I need to know," he answered authoritatively.

Although his air of self-confidence never wavered, I was confused by what he said. Something didn't make sense when you compared the way he looked and the way he talked. So, I pushed for more information about his current situation.

"I'm not working right now. You see, I've had this bad luck of getting stuck working with idiots. They can't do the job right. I try to tell them, even teach them so they can do it right, but they just don't get it! It's so easy for me that I usually end up doing everything myself," Dwayne declared proudly.

With laser-like directness, I asked if he'd quit or been fired.

"It was a draw. You know, mutual on both sides. My boss said I wasn't a team player, and I was ready to go, so we just parted ways."

Then I asked how many jobs he'd had in the last five years.

"He who believes in nobody knows that he himself is not to be trusted."

Berthold Auerbach

2

"Four. You see, I learn fast and then get bored. I just like to move on when I've learned all there is for me in a job," he said, avoiding the real issue.

It quickly became obvious that Dwayne was not only a loner, but a perfectionist. He had real difficulty accepting and dealing with anyone else's shortcomings.

"The Never Good Enough"

Although similar to "The Perfectionist," "The Never Good Enough" has a slightly different approach to Negaholism. She constantly and consistently sets standards and goals that are unattainable. And by setting these unrealistic expectations, she only reinforces the image of herself as a loser.

Profile of "The Never Good Enough"

Georgia is a successful restaurateur in her mid-forties. Attractive, outgoing and fastidious, her clothes are always in style and reveal an artistic bent. She has created an inviting eating environment in an ideal location that offers scrumptious food. Day and night people eagerly line up outside her door waiting to get in.

Despite having all these things going for her, Georgia is not happy. She becomes distraught over a little piece of litter on the floor. She dwells on tardy employees, small mistakes and wrinkled tablecloths. Nothing ever seems good enough for her.

As a result, working for Georgia is frustrating and demoralizing. To make matters worse, she never notices when things are right, such as the food, the customer service, the décor, the location or the atmosphere. She's allowed the minor details that may be wrong to overshadow all the major accomplishments that she should notice and recognize. No matter what she or anyone else does, it's never good enough for Georgia.

"Blessed are those that nought expect, For they shall not be disappointed."

John Walcot

2

"The Slave Driver"

"The Slave Driver" comes from the same Negaholic family as "The Perfectionist" and "The Never Good Enough." He's a bona fide workaholic who compels you to work more, work harder, work smarter — to accomplish one more thing. "The Slave Driver" is definitely all work and no play. He's the kind that sat behind you in college and subconsciously told you to "Write that paper" when you would have preferred to hang out with your friends. Now that you're an adult, he tells you to "Finish that report" when you'd rather take your son to the batting cages.

Profile of "The Slave Driver"

A wiry, slight of build business owner named Len is obsessed with balancing his books. He walks at a fast clip and always seems to have accounting pads stuck under his arms. Len firmly believes that if he doesn't constantly worry over each and every penny his business will go bankrupt. So every time someone asks him to do something fun — like going to the movies or out to dinner — his response is always, "I've got to do the books." In fact, it's become a standard joke to his family, friends and co-workers. "Yeah, Len, I know. You've got to do the books, right?"

> *"All work and no play makes Jack a dull boy."*
>
> James Howell

Exercise: Analyzing Attitudinal Negaholics

Now that you've met the three kinds of Attitudinal Negaholics, answer the following questions.

1. Do you see tendencies of "The Perfectionist" in yourself? If so, how do they show themselves in your words or actions?

   _____

   _____

   _____

2. Do you see tendencies of "The Perfectionist" in any of your family members, friends or co-workers? If so, how do they show themselves in their words or actions?

   _____

   _____

   _____

3. Do you see tendencies of "The Never Good Enough" in yourself? If so, how do they show themselves in your words or actions?

   _____

   _____

   _____

4. Do you see tendencies of "The Never Good Enough" in your family members, friends or co-workers? If so, how do they show themselves in their words or actions?

   _____

   _____

   _____

5. Do you see tendencies of "The Slave Driver" in yourself? If so, how do they show themselves in your words or actions?

_____

_____

_____

6. Do you see tendencies of "The Never Good Enough" in your family members, friends or co-workers? If so, how do they show themselves in their words or actions?

_____

_____

_____

Behavioral Negaholism

It's easy to feel sorry for Behavioral Negaholics because they trip themselves up time and time again. They seem to be "hooked" on their behavior and unable to control or stop it. Generally, they're sweet people that you want to help. But beware. If you get too attached to a Behavioral Negaholic, their problems can become yours. "The Procrastinator," "The Pattern Repeater" and "The Never Measure Up" are specific examples.

"The Procrastinator"

This type of Negaholic puts off everything and can't seem to keep promises. At work, she misses deadlines and conveniently forgets what she commits to do. The story's the same at home. The laundry tends to pile up, and the kids never have what they need for school or other activities. "The Procrastinator" realizes her shortcomings, which only reinforces the fact that she's not up to facing many of life's daily challenges.

> *"Never leave that till tomorrow which you can do today."*
>
> Ben Franklin

Profile of "The Procrastinator"

Paula, a chronic "Procrastinator," is an assistant at a record company. Because of her determined and volatile personality, she defends her procrastinations to the end. Not only does she put things off, but she resists writing them down. This is also compounded by the fact that she's hard of hearing. Needless to say, Paula forgets a lot and lets a lot slip through the cracks.

Her boss is always on her back: "You forgot the light bulbs. Where's the mail? Have you gone to the store? That shipment will be late now!" Each encounter like this either leaves Paula feeling terrible about herself or acting defensive about why she didn't do what she was supposed to do. In addition to experiencing her boss's constant barrage of questions and comments, Paula also hears the same dialogue internally. No wonder she's in a constant state of distress.

"For years I've been saying I'd clean out the garage, but I never seem to get to it. I don't know, at this point, it's a joke. I just can't get things done."

While Paula knows she has a problem with procrastination, she doesn't know what to do about it. In fact, she's come to accept it as part of her personality. But that hasn't stopped her from berating herself or letting others do the same.

"The Pattern Repeater"

Self-sabotage is at the root of this form of Negaholism. Victims repeat the same patterns time after time; they get stuck in ruts they can't get out of. It's almost as if they string a psychological fishing line in front of their paths and then are destined to trip over it, especially as they close in on an important goal.

Profile of "The Pattern Repeater"

Nina came to see me about her weight problem. She wasn't obese, just a little plump. Actually her figure wasn't all that bad, except for her derriere, which was disproportionately large for the rest of her. When she walked, she bent forward slightly so her top half always arrived a step before her bottom half. She spoke in a loud voice and craved constant attention. Although she meant well, she often promised to do things that never got done.

To start with, Nina wanted to lose 15 pounds. She said she was willing to do whatever it would take to drop the weight. I was skeptical of her commitment, but I gave her the benefit of the doubt, and together we designed an acceptable eating plan.

When I asked what other support I could offer, she said, "Remind me if you see me going off track, because I tend to forget. In fact, I'll probably forget what we've talked about today and go against the plan just out of habit."

I agreed to remind her. Unfortunately, I was called to action sooner than I'd hoped. About two hours later I was eating a salad at an outdoor café when I saw Nina stroll by while inhaling a candy bar. I instantly jumped up, darted toward her and asked, "Were you serious about the reminders?"

Embarrassed, she sheepishly answered, "Yes."

"Then maybe you should reconsider your snack," I responded.

Believe it or not, Nina was glad this incident happened. It jolted her out of an automatic behavior and forced her to examine the truth of her words. She began to realize that she was saying one thing and doing another — she was sabotaging herself by engaging in behaviors that went against her wishes and goals. After this realization, Nina proceeded to lose 20 pounds and, as a result, felt stronger, more self-confident and more capable than ever before.

Nina's past behavior is similar to that of another woman I know. Latosha has always struggled with her weight. As she puts it: "My mind wants my body to be thin, but every time I'm around chocolate my hands and mouth act independently. I'm never sure how the chocolate gets into my mouth, but before I know it, it's in my stomach."

> *"Those who fail to learn from their mistakes are destined to repeat them."*

Juan, a stocky, high-energy, workaholic salesman says essentially the same thing using different words and a different situation. "When I plan to take time off from work to be with my family, to go on vacation, to putter in the garden, there's always some emergency that keeps me from getting away. I have the best of intentions, but something inevitably happens."

What's happening with Nina, Latosha and Juan is counter-intention. That means they behave in ways directly opposite of what they really want. It's like playing tennis and visualizing exactly where you want to hit the ball. But instead of hitting the ball in the corner to your opponent's backhand, you aim it right into the net. This counter-intention is the physical manifestation of Negaholism. "Pattern Repeaters" can't get their actions and intentions in synch. And worse yet, they don't know what to do about it.

"The Never Measure Up"

Some people seem to constantly fall short of the mark. The expressions "Always a bridesmaid, never a bride" and "Always in second place" were coined just for them. The satisfaction of being, doing and having exactly what they want is out of their reach. It's as if the cards are stacked against them.

Profile of "The Never Measure Up"

There's always something "off" about Mark's appearance. Tall, dark and disheveled, he either has a button missing, a sock that won't stay up or a cowlick that's out of control. He's a middle-aged bank teller who drives a gray compact car. Secretly he aspires to be a vice president and drive a luxury sedan, but he never quite makes the grade. And deep down inside, he sincerely believes he never will.

"A failure establishes only this, that our determination to succeed was not strong enough."

Christian Nestell Bovee

Exercise: Analyzing Behavioral Negaholics

Now that you've met the three kinds of Behavioral Negaholics, answer the following questions.

1. Do you see tendencies of "The Procrastinator" in yourself? If so, how do they show themselves in your words or actions?

2. Do you see tendencies of "The Procrastinator" in any of your family members, friends or co-workers? If so, how do they show themselves in their words or actions?

3. Do you see tendencies of "The Pattern Repeater" in yourself? If so, how do they show themselves in your words or actions?

4. Do you see tendencies of "The Pattern Repeater" in your family members, friends or co-workers? If so, how do they show themselves in their words or actions?

5. Do you see tendencies of "The Never Measure Up" in yourself? If so, how do they show themselves in your words or actions?

_____

_____

_____

6. Do you see tendencies of "The Never Measure Up" in your family members, friends or co-workers? If so, how do they show themselves in their words or actions?

_____

_____

_____

Mental Negaholism

Perhaps the most subtle and insidious form of Negaholism is Mental Negaholism. Usually these sufferers are completely unaware of their thoughts. They may begin to feel low, withdrawn or in a "funk" and have no idea why. They may transfer these thoughts into actions, or they may keep the thoughts to themselves, living in a private world of self-inflicted punishment. Mental Negaholics include "The Constant Critic," "The Comparing Contestant," "The Retroactive Fault Finder" and "The Premature Invalidator."

"The Constant Critic"

This Negaholic is always down on herself. At times there may be a reason for the criticism — such as losing a major client at work or ending a long-term relationship — while at other times there isn't a logical explanation for it. Bottom line, it's there. Internally, the "Constant Critic" hears "You're so stupid," "You're so incompetent," "You're so ugly," or "You're so unlovable" so much that she begins to believe all of the above. As you might imagine, this represents a more advanced stage of Negaholism.

"It is much easier to be critical than to be correct."

Benjamin Disraeli

Profile of "The Constant Critic"

Arianna is an art director for an advertising agency, where she's worked for 20 years. Lately she's felt she should be making more money at this stage of her career. In fact, she's just come from a job interview, and now, as she walks to her car, she's mulling over how well she did. Her brows are furrowed and her gait uneven as she dodges passers-by. Her mind is on the interview: how she acted, what she said and what her chances are.

Then a voice, seemingly from nowhere, begins to criticize her relentlessly. "You said all the wrong things! You sounded so uncertain, and you didn't list any of your accomplishments. And the way you sat — slumped in your chair. You'll never get the job. You really blew it!"

The critic's constant drone brings Arianna down lower and lower — until she truly believes she's worthless, the situation is hopeless, and any further job-seeking action is pointless.

"The Comparing Contestant"

These Negaholics are always comparing themselves to everyone else. It's probably not surprising that they never measure up. They look at life with a yardstick, as if they were involved in a perpetual contest and under constant scrutiny. For example they tell themselves, "She turned in a great report and mine is just awful," "His golf game is so much better than mine will ever be," "Look at her thighs — they're so much thinner than mine," and "He drives a BMW, and I only have VW."

For "Comparing Contestants," the person who has the most desirable "stuff," the most attractive friends and the seemingly happiest life wins the game. Unfortunately, that's always the other person. This game is about impressing people, having prestige and making everything seem effortless. It's about looking beautiful, making lots of money and being so busy that a simple dinner has to be scheduled

> *"Comparisons are odious."*
>
> Archbishop Boiardo

months in advance. Once started, this game never really ends since there are always new people to measure yourself against and, ultimately, fall short of.

Profile of "The Comparing Contestant"

Brad spends most of his time comparing some aspect of himself to others. For example, he hates the fact that Earl has a brand new BMW, while he's still driving an old VW. Every time he sees Earl, Brad feels envious because an expensive car symbolizes success to him. Brad's comparisons don't stop there. He compares his receding hairline to Hal's full head of hair, his athletic prowess to body-builder Gordon and his job status to Fred, who's on the company's fast track. This judging forces Brad into either a superior or inferior position. And, typically he comes out on the bottom.

"The Retroactive Fault Finder"

A rear-view mirror drives the life of this type of Negaholic. She's constantly looking over her shoulder, dwelling on the past, blowing things out of proportion and belittling herself for irreparable mistakes. Her conversation is littered with "shoulds." "I should not have said that," "I should have sent a birthday card," and "I should have studied harder for the exam." It's obvious this Negaholic is full of regret, remorse and self-recrimination.

Profile of "The Retroactive Fault Finder"

Originally from Switzerland, Clara now lives in California. You'd think that moving to a new country would have given her a chance to make a fresh start. Instead, she can't seem to shake her past. Clara is often heard saying things like, "I never should have left my family," "I should have stayed home and taken care of my mother," "I never should have gone to work for that company," and "I should have gotten a degree in international business." Whatever

"I tell you the past is a bucket of ashes."

Carl Sandburg

Clara's done, it's been wrong, and she can't seem to leave it where it belongs — in the past.

"The Premature Invalidator"

Naturally protective, this Negaholic resists trying new things so he won't be disappointed. On the other hand, he's also poised and ready to pounce on anyone else's mistake.

We all beat ourselves up once in a while for making major blunders. In these cases, a little ranting and raving is probably justified. What isn't justified is berating yourself for a minor mistake. Based upon past performance and a Negative mindset, a "Premature Invalidator" may jump to conclusions and indict himself before reviewing all the facts and the evidence. It's as if he's convicted himself before he's ever been tried. He tells himself "I can't believe that you did that," "You always do that," and "Don't you ever learn?"

Profile of "The Premature Invalidator"

Carlos is a sales representative for an office furniture company. He's been waiting for an important call from a new client most of the morning. Finally around noon, he decides to pick up a sandwich at the corner coffee shop and brings it back to his desk. As luck would have it, during the 15 minutes he's away, the client calls. Immediately, an inner-voice says, "How could you leave the phone, even for a minute? It doesn't matter if you only had coffee for breakfast. Clients come first, not your growling stomach. You're such a screw-up!"

Once Carlos settles down enough to listen to the client's voice-mail message, he realizes it's simply about setting up a face-to-face meeting for later in the week. So there was no real damage done by missing the call. Still Carlos has inflicted damage on himself, and he feels beaten, abused and scarred.

> *"Look before you leap."*
>
> Samuel Butler

Exercise: Analyzing Mental Negaholics

Now that you've met the four kinds of Mental Negaholics, answer the following questions.

1. Do you see tendencies of "The Constant Critic" in yourself? If so, how do they show themselves in your words or actions?

    _____

    _____

    _____

2. Do you see tendencies of "The Constant Critic" in any of your family members, friends or co-workers? If so, how do they show themselves in their words or actions?

    _____

    _____

    _____

3. Do you see tendencies of "The Comparing Contestant" in yourself? If so, how do they show themselves in your words or actions?

    _____

    _____

    _____

4. Do you see tendencies of "The Comparing Contestant" in your family members, friends or co-workers? If so, how do they show themselves in their words or actions?

    _____

    _____

    _____

5. Do you see tendencies of "The Retroactive Fault Finder" in yourself? If so, how do they show themselves in your words or actions?

_____

_____

_____

6. Do you see tendencies of "The Retroactive Fault Finder" in your family members, friends or co-workers? If so, how do they show themselves in their words or actions?

_____

_____

_____

7. Do you see tendencies of "The Premature Invalidator" in yourself? If so, how do they show themselves in your words or actions?

_____

_____

_____

8. Do you see tendencies of "The Premature Invalidator" in your family members, friends or co-workers? If so, how do they show themselves in their words or actions?

_____

_____

_____

Verbal Negaholism

It's in your best interests to stay as far away as possible from a Verbal Negaholic. Just listening to them can deeply depress you or even trigger your own Negattack. That's because they focus only on the Negative, conjure up worst-case scenarios and obsess about everything. For them, gloom and doom aren't just tendencies, they represent a full-time job.

Verbal Negaholics always think of the glass as half empty instead of half full. And because they expect the worst, they typically get it. Their Negativity becomes a self-fulfilling prophecy. For example, you'll often overhear them uttering phrases such as "Just my luck" and "Wouldn't you know it would happen to me."

"The Beartrapper," "The Constant Complainer," "The Heralding Disaster" and "The Gloom and Doomer" are all examples of Verbal Negaholics.

"The Beartrapper"

This Negaholic appears to want help but then rejects it. She may initially seek support, aid, assistance or advice. But when it's offered, there are always excuses: it won't work; it's already been tried; the situation is more complicated than you realize; things are just hopeless.

Also called "Help-Rejecting Complainers," "Beartrappers" get their name from asking other people to help them open their traps of Negativity. Armed with good intentions, these helpers momentarily set their feet in the trap, and it snaps closed. At that point, the helpers become annoyed and angry because they're also caught up in the Negativity.

Profile of "The Beartrapper"

While listening to my friend Carol complain about her husband, I inadvertently got "Beartrapped." Our conversation went something like this:

Carol: Things are really bad.

> *"God helps those who help themselves."*
>
> Algernon Sidney

Cherie: Then maybe it's time to have a talk.

Carol: Oh, he won't talk. He just ignores me every time I try.

Cherie: How about writing him a note and leaving it on the dresser?

Carol: He just throws them in the garbage. He know how much that hurts me.

Cherie: Why don't you call him at the office?

Carol: His secretary knows my voice and won't put me through to him.

Cherie: What about sending him a letter by registered mail?

Carol: I've never tried that, but knowing him he'd never be there to receive it.

Cherie: What about telling him straight out that you've set up an appointment with a marriage counselor and you expect him to be there.

Carol: He'd just laugh at me.

Cherie: All right, you can't talk to him, write him or call him. So why don't you just leave him?

Carol: Because I don't have any money. He controls all the bank accounts, and I only get grocery money. How far would that get me?

Cherie: Why don't you file for divorce?

Carol: It's the money. Lawyers cost money, and I don't have any. The house is in his name and so are the bank accounts, charge cards and all of our assets.

Cherie: Sounds like you're stuck. I just don't know what to tell you.

As you can see, every suggestion I made to Carol was countered. There was always a reason why it wouldn't work. While she appeared to be asking for help, in reality, she wasn't willing to find a solution. She saw her situation as utterly hopeless.

"The Constant Complainer"

Like many addicts, this Negaholic is completely unaware of his condition. He doesn't see, hear or feel his own Negativity because he has a blatant blind spot to anything remotely positive. His Negative attitudes and beliefs are so deeply imbedded inside him that he truly thinks "Life's just like that." He has a complaint about everyone and everything.

Profile of "The Constant Complainer"

Take Nigel, a telemarketing supervisor, as an example. He doesn't understand why co-workers avoid him or why he doesn't have any friends. But it's simply because he's so Negative, nobody wants to hear his never-ending complaints.

If someone suggests a new office filing system, Nigel says, "It will never work." If another supervisor offers a solution to a problem employee's work habits, he injects "She won't do that." If a colleague encourages him to discuss career goals with the telemarketing center manager, he responds "He'll never let me try any of those things." Who wants to be around a person with a Negative attitude like that?

"The Heralding Disaster"

Disaster movies may be popular, but this Negaholic isn't. People quickly tire of hearing about one possible catastrophe after another. Not only does she expect the worst, but she anticipates disasters, tragedies and calamities on a regular basis. She's the one who warns "Oh, no. We're going to have an earthquake and we'll all die!" If things aren't going well at work, she might say, "I'm going to lose my job. Then I won't be able to pay the rent, so I'll be evicted and end up a bag lady on the street — homeless!" Interestingly, research shows that among people's biggest fears is the fear of being homeless.

Profile of "The Heralding Disaster"

Fear is Mary Alice's middle name. This dutiful Midwest housewife who donates much of her time to charities is also busy warning everyone who'll listen about impending disasters. She is intense and dogmatic about her proclamations. For instance, one spring many years ago Mary Alice called all of her friends in California to tell them they should pack up and move to the Midwest.

"California is going to fall into the ocean — the entire coastline all the way from Santa Barbara to San Diego. You must leave before the summer of 1990, or it will be a certain catastrophe," she announced to them in a high-pitched hysterical tone.

At the same time, Mary Alice is also convinced the Midwest will dry up from drought, resulting in crop failure and famine throughout the country and around the world. Of course, according to her, we may all die of terminal diseases or be annihilated by a nuclear attack before that happens. Whatever calamity may occur, Mary Alice wants everyone to be aware of it and prepared for it.

"The Gloom and Doomer"

A first cousin of the "Heralding Disaster" is the "Gloom and Doomer." Although similar, the main difference between the two is that the "Heralding Disaster" focuses on specific events in an urgent, frantic and borderline hysterical manner. All of her statements seem to end in exclamation marks.

In contrast, the "Gloom and Doomer" has a more hopeless tone to his remarks. He doesn't get excited or upset. He's resigned himself to the fact that things won't work out. His mantra is: "It can't be done if it hasn't been done before, so it isn't going to be done now, so why even try?" It was definitely a "Gloom and Doomer" who told the Wright Brothers "If man were meant to fly, God would have given him wings."

> *"All hope abandon, ye who enter here."*
>
> Dante Alighieri

Profile of "The Gloom and Doomer"

Ernie, a production manager at a small manufacturing firm, needed some way to excite his workers about a product they were getting ready to produce. After thinking about it for a few days, he finally decided to give away aqua-colored T-shirts with the company logo on them. Unfortunately, he waited so long to think of his idea that production was only a day away. "It's too bad that we couldn't pull it off. There's just no way we could get those T-shirts produced in one day. It's too bad I didn't think of it sooner," said Ernie regretfully.

Then Ernie began mentally listing all the reasons his great idea wouldn't work. The T-shirt vendor wouldn't have the right color or number of shirts in stock. And, of course, they'd never be able to imprint them with the company logo in such a short timeframe. He gave up on the idea without even checking first. But his secretary didn't. She made a phone call and found out the T-shirts could be produced in less than six hours. Ernie was impressed. Although this incident didn't change his "Gloom and Doom" attitude completely, Ernie did begin to see that some things are possible.

Exercise: Analyzing Verbal Negaholics

Now that you've met the four kinds of Mental Negaholics, answer the following questions.

1. Do you see tendencies of "The Beartrapper" in yourself? If so, how do they show themselves in your words or actions?

   _____

   _____

   _____

2. Do you see tendencies of "The Beartrapper" in any of your family members, friends or co-workers? If so, how do they show themselves in their words or actions?

   _____

   _____

   _____

3. Do you see tendencies of "The Constant Complainer" in yourself? If so, how do they show themselves in your words or actions?

   _____

   _____

   _____

4. Do you see tendencies of "The Constant Complainer" in your family members, friends or co-workers? If so, how do they show themselves in their words or actions?

   _____

   _____

   _____

2

5. Do you see tendencies of "The Heralding Disaster" in yourself? If so, how do they show themselves in your words or actions?

    _____

    _____

    _____

6. Do you see tendencies of "The Heralding Disaster" in your family members, friends or co-workers? If so, how do they show themselves in their words or actions?

    _____

    _____

    _____

7. Do you see tendencies of "The Gloom and Doomer" in yourself? If so, how do they show themselves in your words or actions?

    _____

    _____

    _____

8. Do you see tendencies of "The Gloom and Doomer" in your family members, friends or co-workers? If so, how do they show themselves in their words or actions?

    _____

    _____

    _____

2

Questions for Personal Development

1. What is the major emphasis of this chapter?

   _____

   _____

   _____

2. What are the most important things you learned from this chapter?

   _____

   _____

   _____

3. How can you apply what you learned to your current job?

   _____

   _____

   _____

4. How will you go about making these changes?

   _____

   _____

   _____

5. How can you monitor improvement?

   _____

   _____

   _____

6. Summarize the changes you expect to see in yourself and others one year from now.

   _____

   _____

   _____

2

*C*HAPTER 3

How to Handle Negaholics

In the last chapter we divided Negaholics into four categories: Attitudinal, Behavioral, Mental and Verbal. Although Negativity is at the heart of all their problems, these sufferers think, talk and act it out in very different ways. If you look at all the people you know in your family, at work, in social circles, your neighborhood and your church, you probably know someone who fits just about every Negaholic category.

Negaholism becomes the most challenging in the workplace. Doing your job on a daily basis often requires you to deal with not one but perhaps several different Negaholics. The real challenge is learning how to deal with each one so his Negaholic tendencies are minimized and some real work gets done.

After all, doctors don't treat an infection the same way they do a broken arm. And you shouldn't treat "The Perfectionist" the same way you would "The Beartrapper." They have different problems and different symptoms that require different treatments.

3

*C
A
S
E*

*S
T
U
D
Y*

Case Study: Wayne's Work World

Wayne is a 40-ish, average looking man of average intelligence. His height and weight are also average. His personality is predictable — he's polite but not overly friendly, firm but never stern, very capable but not too ambitious. Almost everything about Wayne, a sales manager, is average except for the fact that he supervises four Negaholics. Needless to say, he has his work cut out for him.

One of Wayne's salespeople, Min, never has a good thing to say about anything or anybody. When Wayne called his group together in December for a goal-setting session for the coming year, Min announced, "This is just a waste of our time. Nobody's going to follow whatever plan we come up with. It'll be forgotten by February!" During the meeting, every time someone suggested an improvement in work processes, Min curtly commented, "Well, that's a stupid idea. It will never work."

In contrast, Mike was eager and enthused about the goal-setting session. He urged everyone to set very high goals for the group — about 20 percent above those for the current year. Wayne thought to himself that a big jump like that might be a little unrealistic. After all, Mike had just been in his office last week complaining that his sales totals weren't as high as he believed they should be.

All the talk during the meeting about higher sales quotas made Marvin nervous. He knew he could never sell as much as the others in the group. It seemed Mike always came out on top, and he was always on the bottom. In fact, Marvin was so obsessed with beating the others that he checked the incoming sales reports every day.

After the meeting, Marla volunteered to type up the notes Wayne had written on a flipchart and to distribute them to everyone in the group. She resolved to get started the next morning. But then something else came up and she forgot about the notes. Finally, a week later, Wayne stopped by to ask about them, so Marla promised they'd be ready by the end of the day. When 5 p.m. rolled around, still no notes. Marla had been sidetracked by yet another project that had fallen through the cracks.

Exercise: Name Those Negaholics

Now that you've met the Negaholics who work for Wayne, answer the following questions:

1. Is Min an Attitudinal, Behavioral, Mental or Verbal Negaholic? What kinds of Negaholic tendencies does she show through her words or actions? Which of the 14 specific Negaholic character types does she most closely resemble?

   _____

   _____

   _____

2. Is Mike an Attitudinal, Behavioral, Mental or Verbal Negaholic? What kinds of Negaholic tendencies does he show through his words or actions? Which of the 14 specific Negaholic character types does he most closely resemble?

   _____

   _____

   _____

3. Is Marvin an Attitudinal, Behavioral, Mental or Verbal Negaholic? What kinds of Negaholic tendencies does he show through his words or actions? Which of the 14 specific Negaholic character types does he most closely resemble?

   _____

   _____

   _____

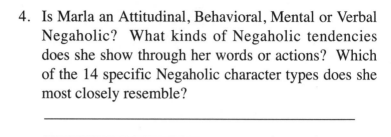

4. Is Marla an Attitudinal, Behavioral, Mental or Verbal Negaholic? What kinds of Negaholic tendencies does she show through her words or actions? Which of the 14 specific Negaholic character types does she most closely resemble?

_____

_____

_____

You'll revisit Wayne, Min, Mike, Marvin and Marla in the next chapter. Just for the record, Min is a "Constant Complainer" (Verbal Negaholic); Mike is a "Never Good Enough" (Attitudinal Negaholic); Marvin is a "Comparing Contestant" (Mental Negaholic); and Marla is a "Procrastinator" (Behavioral Negaholic).

Negaholic Coping Strategies

There are four basic steps you need to follow in order to cope with any type of Negaholic.

1. **Determine how pervasive the syndrome is.** Remember that people are affected by different levels of Negaholism. Some have slight cases, some have moderate cases, and others suffer from full-blown Negattacks on a regular basis.
2. **Note the different forms it takes.** How do the person's words and actions indicate that he's a Negaholic?
3. **Group your Negaholic.** Based on your observations of the person's words and actions, is he an Attitudinal, Behavioral, Mental or Verbal Negaholic?
4. **Strategize how to deal with your Negaholic.** Obviously, this will vary according to the type of Negaholic you've identified.

Coping Strategies for Attitudinal Negaholics

You may recall this is the most subtle form of Negaholism because everything looks fine on the surface. This Negaholic appears very clean, orderly and controlled. Underneath, however, he's relentlessly driven and tormented by unachievable perfection. Here are four steps to deal with him:

1. **Recognize that this person suffers from a self-esteem problem.** He may seem perfect on the outside, but he's full of insecurities on the inside.
2. **Put a stop to any self-diminishment the minute you hear it.** Don't allow him to say Negative things about himself. Interrupt him immediately.
3. **Validate his achievements.** Highlight all the good things he's done and continues to do.
4. **Focus on his positive characteristics.** Turn his Negative words and actions into positive ones. This shouldn't be difficult since an Attitudinal Negaholic actually has a lot going for him.

For example, Wayne realizes Mike is a classic "Never Good Enough" Attitudinal Negaholic. He constantly pushes himself to do more, to do better because of a deeply imbedded self-esteem problem. No matter how hard he tries or how well he does, Mike is never satisfied with his efforts.

When Mike privately complained to Wayne that his sales totals were falling short of his own expectations, Wayne quickly assured Mike that he was very pleased with his results. Then they went over some of the figures together, with Wayne pointing out some of the most positive examples. By the time Mike left Wayne's office a half-hour later, he felt a lot better about himself and his achievements.

3

Coping Strategies for Behavioral Negaholics

Self-sabotage and overindulgence are the telltale marks of these Negaholics. They subconsciously set themselves up for a fall and then act out their Negativity through excessive working, drinking, eating, gossiping, and time-wasting or through abusing drugs. All of these things can affect work productivity and performance. So when confronting a Behavioral Negaholic follow these three guidelines:

1. **Recognize that this person sabotages himself by engaging in overindulgent behavior.** He may seem to enjoy whatever he overdoes, but this couldn't be farther from the truth.

2. **Bring the overindulgent behavior to his attention.** Make your comments in a gentle, nonthreatening, matter-of-fact way.

3. **Focus on a positive step that forces the person out of his Negative behavior.** Suggest that he try doing something else in place of the overindulgent behavior, such as drinking a glass of water or a diet drink instead of eating a candy bar.

It's obvious to Wayne, for example, that Marla shows all the symptoms of a "Procrastinator" Behavioral Negaholic. She routinely puts off projects to the very last minute. As a result, she often misses deadlines and makes too many careless mistakes. However, she means well and typically works late to straighten things out.

When Marla failed to type up the notes from the goal-setting meeting on time, Wayne called her into his office. He patiently and sensitively explained that she wouldn't have to work so late every night if she organized her time better. He even offered to send her to a time-management course. In the meantime, he suggested that Marla make a to-do list at the end of each workday. That way the next morning she would know exactly what needed to be accomplished. Marla seemed pleased with Wayne's suggestions. She left his office resolved to start her to-do list immediately.

3

Coping Strategies for Mental Negaholics

This Negaholic constantly flogs himself for something he's said or done in the past. He lives in a world of criticism, judgments, invalidation and mental abuse, all of which are self-inflicted. And he often translates his Negaholic thoughts into Negaholic actions. When dealing with a Mental Negaholic, try these four steps:

1. **Recognize that this person suffers from a self-esteem problem.** He can't seem to stop rubbing salt in his own wounds.
2. **Put a stop to any self-inflicted Negative comments the minute you hear them.** Try to break the constant cycle of mental abuse.
3. **Validate his past achievements.** Since he's so obsessed with past wrongs, point out what he's done right or done well in the past.
4. **Help him focus on a positive future.** He'll never be able to right past wrongs, but he can learn from his mistakes and vow not to repeat them.

As a "Comparing Contestant," Marvin berates himself and his abilities by constantly comparing himself to others. For example, he's convinced he'll never beat Mike in the monthly sales contest. Even if he has a good week, he can't seem to enjoy it because he's consumed by how the others are doing.

Wayne has noticed Marvin's obsession and is working with him to overcome it. Anytime he hears Marvin say something Negative about his performance, Wayne makes sure he interjects something positive in its place. He also takes time to meet with Marvin every couple of days to give him a pep talk and to review his sales figures, carefully avoiding any comparisons with his colleagues. Wayne's also suggested that Marvin track his own performance by setting weekly sales quotas for himself and then keeping a chart to show his actual weekly sales totals.

3

Coping Strategies for Verbal Negaholics

Your first inclination is to run as far away as possible from a Verbal Negaholic. Listening to him can either drive you crazy or trigger your own Negaholic tendencies. Focusing on the Negative or highlighting the worst-case scenario is his full-time preoccupation. Make sure you maintain a sense of humor or keep things in perspective if you spend much time around a Verbal Negaholic. Also try these four suggestions:

1. **Recognize that this person suffers from a thoroughly Negative attitude.** He is so consumed by Negativity that it's almost impossible for him to think in any other ways.

2. **Try to divert his attention away from Negative words and actions.** This may seem impossible, but when he starts on a Negative tirade, ignore what he's saying and move on to another subject. Hopefully, he'll get the message that you don't want to be part of his Negattack.

3. **Help him recall positives from the past.** Talk about past events or outcomes that have gone well or turned out better than he originally expected.

4. **Help him focus on positives in the future.** Talk about how you can ensure that future events and outcomes are positive.

In many ways, Wayne considers Min, a "Constant Complainer," his greatest challenge. Because she never has a good thing to say about anything or anybody, it's difficult for him and others to be around her for any length of time. Still, he's committed to helping her turn her attitude around.

During the next group meeting, when Min began criticizing her clients, Wayne quickly shut her off by asking for her input on a proposed new order-taking procedure. Of course, Min eagerly stepped in with her Negative comments. Instead of letting her drone on, Wayne asked her to state what she thought worked well in the current procedure.

3

Then he went a step further by asking her to state what she'd like to see included in the new procedure. This forced Min to think in a positive way rather than a Negative way.

Exercise: Coping With Your Negaholics

Apply the strategies you've learned to the Negaholics in your life — either on or off the job by completing this exercise. It's important that you recognize different kinds of Negaholism and put a stop to them — or at the very least slow them down — before they spread.

1. Identify an Attitudinal Negaholic in your life and formulate a strategy for dealing with his Negativity.

   _____

   _____

   _____

2. Identify a Behavioral Negaholic in your life and formulate a strategy for dealing with his Negativity.

   _____

   _____

   _____

3. Identify a Mental Negaholic in your life and formulate a strategy for dealing with his Negativity.

   _____

   _____

   _____

4. Identify a Verbal Negaholic in your life and formulate a strategy for dealing with his Negativity.

   _____

   _____

   _____

3

Questions for Personal Development

1. What is the major emphasis of this chapter?

   _____

   _____

   _____

2. What are the most important things you learned from this chapter?

   _____

   _____

   _____

3. How can you apply what you learned to your current job?

   _____

   _____

   _____

4. How will you go about making these changes?

   _____

   _____

   _____

5. How can you monitor improvement?

   _____

   _____

   _____

6. Summarize the changes you expect to see in others one year from now.

   _____

   _____

   _____

CHAPTER 4

Negaholism and Its Effect on Teams

You've seen how Negaholism can adversely impact the workplace. Now imagine how bad things could be with a whole team of Negaholics.

Their tendencies could contaminate everything they try to do or everyone they come in contact with.

As an example, let's revisit Wayne's goal-setting meeting from the last chapter. For starters, Marla shows up late for the meeting and, instead of participating, finishes some unrelated paperwork that should have been turned in two days ago. Meantime, Mike tries to persuade everyone to set unrealistic sales goals, while Marvin whines that he'll never be able to compete with his co-workers' results. And, of course, no matter what anyone says, Min cuts it down.

This is a classic case of Team Negaholism. Any energy in the room evaporates, hopelessness fills the air, and team members become apathetic. The virus may start with one individual and then spread from person to person, until the entire team of usually competent, capable and intelligent people turn into helpless, hapless and dull-witted dolts.

4

Negaholic Team Behaviors

When a team takes on a Negative attitude, look for specific signs from individual team members. Ask yourself these questions:

- Do team members compete rather than collaborate?
- Do team members appear to operate autonomously rather than cooperatively?
- Do team members have ambiguous, if not strained, relationships?
- Do team members blame each other when things go wrong?
- Do team members bicker and quarrel over what seems like trivial or childish issues?
- Do team members appear isolated and pitted against each other by managers and department heads?
- Do team members seem to not trust each other?
- Do team members experience breakdowns in communication that result in vital information intentionally being withheld or not shared?
- Do team members dwell on reasons, excuses, explanations and justifications rather than address needed solutions?
- Do team members display inconsistencies in direction, strategies, policies or procedures?
- Do team members have different or conflicting goals from other departments or divisions?

If you answered yes to any of these questions about your team or one you supervise, then heed that as a warning sign. If you don't take action now, you'll end up with an entire team of "I can'ts" or Negaholics. No real work will get done. Your team will deteriorate due to three factors:

1. **A lack of creativity.** Team members need fresh ideas to keep them interested, alert and enthusiastic.
2. **Diminished morale.** If poor morale is a problem, team members may feel so demoralized that they just give up.

3. **Disempowerment.** When team members believe they can't make a difference, then they won't even want to try.

Several years ago I met with one company's employees and asked them if their sales and service departments worked together effectively. My inquiry was answered by a roomful of incredulous looks and this response: "This is historic. Sales and service here are like oil and water. They just don't mix."

This belief had embedded itself into the organization. No one questioned it because it had become the norm. After several more meetings in which I described, explained and identified Negaholic behaviors, the employees finally began to see the light. They realized their Negative beliefs were so pervasive that they were oblivious to them. Only after this realization did things start to turn around for the company.

What this example proves is that teams must be made aware of and then accept the fact they have Negaholic tendencies before any change can occur. Awareness and acceptance are both critical to the healing process. It doesn't matter what kind of team you're on or supervise; it doesn't matter what business or industry you're in. If Negaholism exists within a team or among differing teams, you're waging a war that no one wins.

Change and Negativity

In today's fast-paced world of downsizing, rightsizing, reorganizing, re-engineering and outsourcing, you can count on one constant: change. Ironic, isn't it?

People naturally resist change. They typically like things that are familiar and predictable. But bottom line, they need to adjust to it in order to survive and thrive in today's workplace. That goes for teams, too.

4

There are two basic types of change:

1. **Intrinsic change.** This is the kind you choose — the kind that comes from within you. You're in the driver's seat so to speak. Your team decides to rewrite the company's hiring policy, reorganize the office files or restructure the data processing department.

2. **Extrinsic change.** This is the kind you can't choose — the kind that's forced upon you. In this case, changes in the company's hiring policy, office filing system or data processing department are beyond your control. Your team is informed of the changes and must adapt accordingly.

Either kind of change — intrinsic or extrinsic — brings stress, which can result in fear, doubt and even panic. Team members may also suffer from feelings of confusion, uncertainty, anxiety, isolation and unmotivation. They may appear overwhelmed, out of control and unable to perform. This is best represented by the following equation:

Change + Stress + "I Can't" Syndrome = Negaholism

In some cases, team members may resist change. You can hear their Negaholism in comments like these:

- "No one asked me."
- "No one cares what I think."
- "I'm not important."
- "I didn't ask for this."
- "I don't have a choice."
- "There's no way I'm going along with this."
- "I'll show them. I'm going to resist or sabotage this change."

4

Exercise: Changing Times on Your Team

Answer the following questions as they apply to your team.

1. What kind of intrinsic change has your team experienced?

   _____

   _____

   _____

2. How did team members react to the change?

   _____

   _____

   _____

3. What kind of extrinsic change has your team experienced?

   _____

   _____

   _____

4. How did team members react to the change?

   _____

   _____

   _____

4

How to Take the Negativity Out of Teams

As I said before, Negaholism is like a contagious virus that spreads from person to person. And it only takes one person exhibiting Negaholic tendencies to start a full-blown epidemic. So keep your eye out for the telltale symptoms previously mentioned. If you suspect any Negaholism, take these three steps:

1. **Establish clear roles and responsibilities.** Make sure team members understand what's expected of them in terms of preparation, participation and product output.

For example, one fast-track company in Silicon Valley equips all of its employees with a state-of-the-art backpack containing a laptop computer, cellular telephone and a pager. Employees are expected to stay in touch and stay connected with the home office no matter where they are or what they're doing. Mostly importantly, this message is stressed to employees from the minute they're hired.

2. **Set clear ground rules.** Explain to team members what behavior is acceptable on the job and especially during team meetings. Tell and show them how to properly participate.

An insurance company that used to suffer from team Negativity set these simple ground rules: no interrupting, no attacking or defending fellow team members, no problems unless accompanied by possible solutions and no knocking other's ideas. In the past, these team members jockeyed for position — they all wanted to be right, and each wanted to find the perfect solution. But their wishes weren't compatible with successful team behavior. Setting ground rules forced them to behave in more acceptable ways.

Remember, once you establish ground rules, you also have to determine what will happen when someone breaks them. And it's only a matter of time before someone will. Here are two suggestions for dealing with the inevitable.

- **Put one person in charge of enforcing the ground rules.** The Sergeant-at-Arms, if you will. (Unless one person really enjoys this job, you may want to rotate it periodically.) Make it this person's responsibility to inform the rule-breaker of her infraction.
- **Establish a consequence for those who break the rules.** For instance, if one team member interrupts another, she might have to contribute one dollar to the team-building activities fund.

Ground rules are a great way to prevent or eliminate Negaholism on your team. But simply having rules isn't the solution. You have to enforce them and have definite consequences in place when they're broken. This will help keep your team on track and moving in the right direction.

3. **Bring structure to team activities.** Structure adds clarity, purpose and organization to whatever your team needs or wants to do. This may be as simple as having an agenda and a specific time frame for a team meeting or as complex as scheduling training time for 20 different team members.

Team Negaholism seems to show itself in one of two ways: either during meetings or when members interact one-on-one. Obviously, it's easier to control during meetings since you can observe individuals and their group dynamics. If someone displays a lack of respect, support or compromise, you can address the problem immediately and move on. Hopefully the lessons learned during these meetings will carry over to the one-on-one interactions.

**C
A
S
E

S
T
U
D
Y**

Case Study: Wayne's Work World

Wayne decides to take action to stop Negaholism from overrunning his team. First, he establishes clear roles and responsibilities for members by meeting with each one individually. He tells each person how valuable he or she is to the team's success, and then together they determine realistic, yet challenging sales quotas for the next few months. Because of differences in personalities, experience and clients, not everyone on the team is given the same quota.

Second, Wayne calls a meeting to set clear ground rules for team interaction. Each item on his list addresses a Negaholic characteristic of at least one of his team members. Here's Wayne's list:

- Respect each other's ideas and abilities. (Min)
- Respect your own ideas and abilities. (Mike, Marvin)
- Consider all ideas and points of view. (Min)
- Work together as a team, not as individual competitors. (Everyone, but especially Marvin)
- Meet commitments on time and to the best of your abilities. (Everyone, but especially Marla)

Initially, Wayne chooses Mike to enforce the ground rules, although he eventually plans to rotate this assignment. Together the group decides that anyone who breaks the rules will have to bring donuts to the next team meeting. As for bringing structure to team activities, Wayne is already doing that. His meetings always begin on time, never last more than an hour and have a specific agenda.

Wayne feels he's made a positive step toward eliminating some of the Negativity from his team, but he knows there's a long way to go. A truly healthy and non-Negaholic team exhibits these important characteristics:

- Competence
- Good communication
- Certainty

- Integrity
- Trust
- Participation from all team members
- Leadership from all team members
- Ownership of problems
- A willingness to compromise

If you see these characteristics at work in your team meetings and when team members work together, consider yourself lucky. You've nipped the Negaholism in the bud.

Exercise: Taking the Negativity Out of Your Team

Answer the following questions as they apply to your team.

1. How would you establish clear roles and responsibilities for your team?

   _____
   _____
   _____

2. What clear ground rules would you set?

   _____
   _____
   _____

3. Who should be put in charge of enforcing the ground rules?

   _____
   _____
   _____

4. What consequences should be established for breaking the rules?

   _____
   _____
   _____

5. How can you bring structure to team activities?

_____

_____

_____

6. What characteristics does your team currently exhibit?

_____

_____

_____

Questions for Personal Development

1. What is the major emphasis of this chapter?

_____

_____

_____

2. What are the most important things you learned from this chapter?

_____

_____

_____

3. How can you apply what you learned to your current job?

_____

_____

_____

4. How will you go about making these changes?

_____

_____

_____

5. How can you monitor improvement?

_____

_____

_____

6. Summarize the changes you expect to see in your team one year from now.

_____

_____

_____

4

4

CHAPTER 5

Confronting Your Own Negaholism

Perhaps it's not your employees, your boss or your teammates who are the source of Negativity in the workplace. Perhaps it's you. Admitting you're a Negaholic is one of the hardest things you'll ever do. But you'll never recover if you don't first admit you have a problem.

Back in Chapter One, you completed The Negaholic Self-Assessment Tool. That should have given you a pretty clear picture of where you fit on the Negativity scale. Virtually all of us show Negaholic tendencies now and then. Whether you have a mild case or suffer from something more severe, now is the time to confront it once and for all.

How You Handle Change and Stress

Remember what I said about change in the last chapter: People naturally resist it, preferring things that are familiar and predictable. This rule applies to you, too. You may think you accept and even welcome change, but in most cases you offer at least some resistance. It may be subconscious, but it's there.

When you experience change, you also experience stress. You may feel tense, overwhelmed and ready to lash out at anyone who pushes you too far. The "I can't self" takes over, and you may hear yourself saying things like:

> *"We must adjust to changing times and still hold to unchanging principles."*
>
> Jimmy Carter

- "I can't (or won't) do it!"
- "I can't take it!"
- "It will never work."
- "It's impossible."
- "It's too difficult."
- "It's not feasible."
- "That's not the way we do business."
- "That's not who we are."
- "We've always done it this way before."
- "It's never been done before."
- "They won't go for it."

Once you reach this point, you're close to a full-blown Negattack.

Remember this equation from the last chapter:

Change + Stress + "I Can't" Syndrome = Negaholism

How did you reach this point? Following are some clues that stress may be bombarding you from more sides than you can handle. Note how many of these stress-inducing situations apply to your professional or personal life.

- Health-related problems (either you or a loved one)
- Child care concerns
- Adding or losing family members (birth, marriage, death)
- A job change (promotion, downsizing or workload increase)
- A financial change
- Moving (home or office)
- Changes in eating habits, sleep patterns or commuting
- Starting or ending school

Exercise: Evaluating the Stress in Your Life

Think about the life events — such as the ones listed above — that you've experienced both personally and professionally during the past five years. List each one and then determine how much stress each caused you. How did you handle the stress at the time? Was there a better way you could have dealt with it?

5

_____

_____

_____

_____

_____

_____

_____

_____

_____

_____

Negaholics typically react to change and stress in three ways:

1. **They cling to the old and familiar ways of doing things.** It's like having to get rid of an old, comfortable yet worn pair of shoes. You put it off as long as possible. Or, if you're old enough, you might remember when desktop computers began to replace typewriters. A lot of employees resisted learning how to use the new-fangled machines and opted to keep their typewriters close by.

2. **They deny things are changing.** Many of those same employees believed computers would never last. They thought it was a waste of time to learn something totally new when typewriters were sure to make a comeback. (Guess who had the last laugh?) Or, in the case of those old shoes, you may be so attached to them that you overlook the holes in the toes or the paper-thin soles.

3. **They appear unwilling or resistant to change.** As I've said before, people naturally resist change until it's forced on them. For instance, you may refuse to throw away the old shoes. Then one day your spouse does it when you're away from home. By the time you realize they're gone, it's too late. The same thing happed with the typewriters. The company eventually decided they had to go too since they'd outlived their usefulness. Only then did the resistant employees reluctantly adapt to computers.

Getting to the Heart of Your Negaholic Issues

All kinds of thoughts and feelings contribute to your Negaholism. That's especially true at work, where you come in contact with many different personalities, projects, procedures and protocols. By nature, the workplace is a high-stress environment.

When your stress level begins to soar, look inward for signs of these thoughts and feelings:

- Abandonment, rejection, feelings of being unwanted or unloved or unworthy
- Disillusionment, disenchantment, disappointment, deception
- Fear, suspicion, anxiety, concern about integrity, lack of trust or faith
- Loss, separation, involuntary distancing, lack of a connection
- Loss of control or autonomy, powerlessness
- Struggles with authority figures
- Self-criticism, feeling incapable or inadequate or imperfect or judged
- Dependence on others to meet your needs
- Feeling responsible or taking blame for unacceptable outcomes
- Lack of well-established ground rules and boundaries for preferred behavior
- The desire to be liked: having your self-worth dependent on other people's opinions

These thoughts and feelings tend to pop up when you believe you have no say in your life — when things are beyond your control. In other words, when you have no choice. Everything positive seems to evaporate, and Negativity floods your entire being.

Then you start sending yourself messages like these: "No one cares what I think or feel. My opinions aren't valued. I'm not included in the decision-making process. I'm simply told what to do. Well, I'll show them. I'll exercise my power by resisting or sabotaging their change. I won't give in without a fight!"

Those are pretty strong words. They should serve as a warning signal that your Negativity is out of control. If this happens to you, take these actions:

5

- **Regain your control.** Focus on any positives you can identify in your life. For example, create a personal "balance sheet." On one side of a piece of paper write down "What's working," and on the other write down "What's not working." Compare the two. You might be surprised to find there are more good things going on in your life than you originally thought.

- **Exercise your right to choose.** Whenever possible, make choices concerning the things you can control. Put yourself in the driver's seat of life. This will help you reclaim your independence, confidence and sense of power and control. Remember, refusing or being reluctant to make a choice is a choice in and of itself. Procrastinating, delaying and avoiding will never get you what you want.

- **Seek solutions to your stressors.** Get to the root of what's causing your stress. Again, take a piece of paper and write "What's on my mind" at the top. List everything Negative — everything that's bothering you — on the left side of the paper. Then draw a line down the middle. On the right side, list at least one action step you can take to eliminate it.

- **Avoid being overwhelmed.** Sometimes this will be beyond your own control, especially at work. However, if you feel you have more on your plate than you can handle, tell someone who can do something about it. Let your boss know it's a struggle for you to meet all of your responsibilities. It's in everybody's best interests — yours, your boss's and your organization's — for you to stay healthy mentally and physically. (Remember, stress can cause illnesses, too.) If you feel overwhelmed in your personal life, do something about it. You do have control here. Cut out some activities, delegate household chores and find time to relax and enjoy life.

5

- **Enable rather than unable.** Get out there and do things you've always wanted to do, but thought you couldn't do. Enroll in night classes to further your career, learn to play golf or take up painting. Find ways to empower yourself and reinforce your self-confidence.

- **Reach out for support.** You don't have to go through this alone. There are support groups and hotlines for just about every kind of problem. Check your telephone directory, local newspaper or even the Internet for contact numbers and more information. Talk about your problem with someone you trust -- whether it's a family member, friend, a member of the clergy, your supervisor or a professional counselor. You don't have to go through this alone.

When Negaholism gains control over your life, you feel as if you've hit bottom. Keep in mind, though, there's only one way to go: up. The first step is always admitting you have a problem. Only then can you take the next steps to pull yourself out of the pit of total Negativity.

5

Exercise: My Personal "Balance Sheet"

As suggested in this chapter, make two lists in the space below. On the left side write "What's working in my life," and on the right side write "What's not working in my life." Then compare the two lists.

My Personal "Balance Sheet"

What's working in my life　　　**What's not working in my life**

Exercise: What's on My Mind

Again, here's a suggested exercise from this chapter. In the left column, write all the Negatives you perceive in your life. Then, in the right column, write at least one positive action step you can take to overcome each Negative.

What's on My Mind

Perceived Negatives   **Positive Action Steps**

Questions for Personal Development

1. What is the major emphasis of this chapter?

   _____
   _____
   _____

2. What are the most important things you learned from this chapter?

   _____
   _____
   _____

3. How can you apply what you learned to your current job or your personal life?

   _____
   _____
   _____

4. How will you go about making these changes?

   _____
   _____
   _____

5. How can you monitor improvement?

   _____
   _____
   _____

6. Summarize the changes you expect to see in yourself one year from now.

   _____
   _____
   _____

CHAPTER 6

Negaholism on the Job

In this chapter, we'll take a closer look at how Negaholism affects the workplace, specifically your co-workers and your company's teams. Let's start by taking another test, The Negaholism Assessment Tool for Companies.

The Negaholic Assessment Tool for Companies

Answer yes or no to each of the following 28 questions.

YES   NO 1. Do individuals from one work group, department, division, or subsidiary regularly talk about people from other work groups, departments, divisions or subsidiaries in a snide, cynical or sarcastic manner?

YES   NO 2. Do top managers from different work groups, departments, divisions and subsidiaries avoid each other?

YES   NO 3. Is there an unhealthy competition being waged among these top managers?

6

YES NO 4. Do some work groups, departments, divisions or subsidiaries seem to have differing or conflicting goals?

YES NO 5. Are these differences and conflicts among work groups, departments, divisions or subsidiaries swept under the carpet because people are unable or unwilling to address them?

YES NO 6. Is pertinent information or knowledge being withheld from a work group, department, division or subsidiary that could benefit from having it?

YES NO 7. Do work groups, departments, divisions or subsidiaries seem to bicker and quarrel over trivial issues?

YES NO 8. Are people in these work groups, departments, divisions or subsidiaries competing rather than cooperating?

YES NO 9. Is there a duplication of resources because of a lack of cooperation?

YES NO 10. Do these work groups, departments, divisions or subsidiaries blame each other and point fingers at each other over differing issues and concerns?

YES NO 11. Are the relationships among these work groups, departments, divisions and subsidiaries mostly antagonistic in nature?

YES NO 12. Do you notice that secrets are kept among these work groups, departments, divisions and subsidiaries, which are inappropriate and guarded?

YES NO 13. Have you observed an environment of mistrust among these work groups, departments, divisions and subsidiaries?

YES NO 14. Is there a lack of alignment among the leaders and managers of these work groups,

6

departments, divisions and subsidiaries?

YES   NO 15. Are there certain topics that should never be addressed in front of certain individuals from specific work groups, departments, divisions and subsidiaries?

YES   NO 16. Do employees from one work group, department, division or subsidiary think that employees in another are all incompetent?

Do you observe that managers and department, division and subsidiary heads are ...

YES   NO 17. Motivated by ends and not the means?

YES   NO 18. Spending too much of their time talking about other work groups, departments, divisions or subsidiaries?

YES   NO 19. Engaged in devising strategies for border skirmishes?

YES   NO 20. Focused on winning their own battles but not contributing to the big picture?

Do you notice people in these work groups, departments, divisions or subsidiaries operating out of ...

YES   NO 21. Secrecy?

YES   NO 22. Subterfuge?

YES   NO 23. Conspiracy?

YES   NO 24. Sabotage?

YES   NO 25. Undermining behavior?

YES   NO 26. A desire to back stab?

YES   NO 27. A desire to set people up for failure?

YES   NO 28. Collusion?

6

Scoring: Give your company 4 points for every YES answer. Then total your points and find your company on the scale below.

0   Congratulate yourself for being part of a healthy and highly functional organization. You should look forward to a productive and satisfying future there.

1-30   This score indicates a mild case of Negaholism. While your work environment isn't ideal, it's still functional and relatively healthy. If you take the initiative and assume a leadership role, you could help your organization become even healthier. But the organization also must make a commitment to overcoming its Negative tendencies. Several team-building sessions should help.

30-70   This score indicates your organization has strong Negaholic tendencies. If addressed now, many of these issues could be resolved. However, if left unaddressed, they will grow into a chronic condition and eventually they could lead to a company-wide epidemic. Sooner or later the Negaholism will affect the organization's bottom line. A good first step to reverse this trend would be a meeting of all department, division and subsidiary heads. The next step would be a full diagnosis of the situation. (The Negaholic Assessment Tool for Companies may be helpful here.) Your organization also may want to hire an organizational change agent or consultant to help with this and to design some much needed team-building activities.

70-112 Your organization needs to take its situation very seriously. If not addressed now, it is destined to become an organization mired in

Negaholism. At this point, things have already entered the danger zone. To start turning around the situation these steps must be taken immediately. First, determine how widespread the situation is. (Again, you may want to use this assessment tool.) Second, plan a course of action, formulating a statement of purpose, a mission statement and a list of goals and objectives. Among the issues you'll need to address are decision-making, leadership, values, priorities, structure, training, interpersonal dynamics and organizational culture. A master plan like this will ensure that all issues are addressed in a methodical fashion. Contracting with an organizational change agent or consultant also will help.

The building block of any organization — whether it scores high or low on the Negaholic scale — is its employees. The truth is most people want to do a good job. They want to use their skills, abilities and talents for the good of the organization. They also want to be appreciated, compensated and rewarded for their efforts.

Finding the Right People for the Job

If you really want to prevent Negaholism from running amuck in your organization, then take a long look at your employees. Their attitudes and actions have a big effect on the attitude and action of your organization. And vice versa.

The best place to start is your hiring process. If you hire the right people in the first place, then you'll never have to worry about Negaholism gaining a toehold in your organization.

During the interviewing and screening phases, it's essential that you not only find qualified candidates but also motivated ones. In fact, research shows that motivation may

"The laborer is worthy of his hire."

Luke 10:7

6

77

be a better indicator of job success than proven skills. According to studies, people who possess skills without motivation are actually less likely to deliver a quality work product. However, motivated people who don't possess the necessary skills are more likely to learn what's required to do the job well.

So, when hiring potential employees, look for these three things:

1. **Skills and abilities**. Make sure the candidate has the skills you need or that he has the capacity to learn them. Many companies large and small regularly test job candidates before, during and after their interviews. Testing like this often weeds out unsuitable candidates.

Take Ted, who seemed so enthusiastic, positive and eager that he was hired for a sales representative's job despite not being computer literate or having any sales experience. Rather than talking to his boss about his skill deficiencies or seeking help from other sources, Ted became withdrawn and Negative and lost all enthusiasm for his new career. Eventually, he lost his job, too. Just because he appeared positive and eager during the interview didn't mean Ted would automatically learn or adapt to his new position. A series of tests during the hiring process might have alerted his boss to this possibility.

2. **Motivation to do the job.** Be certain the candidate really wants this job, not another one. Is he just trying to get his foot in the door so he can apply for the position he really wants in a couple of months? Or is he settling for this job until something better comes along? You need to feel confident that he's excited and motivated to perform this job with both pride and excellence. During the interview you should be able to detect the candidate's enthusiasm, energy and passion. He'll give you clues you can see, hear and feel. For instance, does he have a sparkle in his eye, a lilt in his voice and positive

"vibes" emanating from his body? If so, you've probably found your man (or woman).

Jamal is a perfect example of why motivation is such an important factor to consider during the hiring process. While he is totally qualified to be a customer service representative — and actually quite good at it — Jamal hates his job and makes sure everyone knows it. It isn't a good fit with his true interests — art, painting and sculpture. He simply does the customer service rep's job to pay the bills since he can't make a living doing what he really loves. As a result, one unhappy yet qualified apple is spoiling it for everyone else.

3. **Cultural fit in the organization.** The job candidate needs to feel comfortable and at ease in your organization. Remember the old saying, "You can't fit a square peg into a round hole"? That logic applies here. If the candidate's personality doesn't come close to that of other employees, chances are she'll eventually quit or be fired. To avoid this situation, look for clues during the interview. For example, does she say "I" more often or "we" more often? Someone who emphasizes "I" may not be a good fit for a team-oriented organization. Does she seem to prefer autonomy and freedom over teamwork and communication? Pay attention to this or again you may have a mismatch. Also ask about her aspirations for the future. Does your organization offer opportunities that will allow her to grow personally and professionally? If not, you probably should look at other job candidates.

An accounting firm learned that the hard way when it hired Theresa for its data processing department. Most accountants prefer to work strictly by the book, with specific hours, procedures and protocols in place. In contrast, Theresa liked to do things her way. She often came in late and left early. She dressed more casually than everyone else did. She tended to skip meetings, training sessions and even the office Christmas party. Bottom line, she didn't fit the culture of an accounting firm. It was only a matter of time before the company let her go.

Exercise: Evaluating Your Organization's Hires

Think about the people you've hired within your organization. Or if you don't have that responsibility, think of some of the employees others have hired. Rate them on a scale of 1 to 10 — 10 being the highest — in each of the following categories. Then determine why you rated them the way you did.

1. Skills and abilities

- Employee: _____ Rating: _____

- Employee: _____ Rating: _____

- Employee: _____ Rating: _____

2. Motivation to do the job

- Employee: _____ Rating: _____

- Employee: _____ Rating: _____

- Employee: _____ Rating: _____

3. Cultural fit in the organization

- Employee: _____ Rating: _____

- Employee: _____ Rating: _____

- Employee: _____ Rating: _____

Making the Most of a Job Interview

In preparation for an interview, you typically scan the person's resume for nuggets of useful information. Unfortunately, a resume focuses almost exclusively on past accomplishments. It tells you what the candidate did in previous jobs, not what you can expect her to do in this job.

Furthermore, resumes usually overlook important issues such as future career goals and objectives for personal development. As a result, you need to draw these out of the candidate yourself during the interview. Here are some specific examples of questions to ask.

- What motivates or drives the candidate to achieve and succeed?
- What things are important to the candidate? Money? Promotions? Recognition?
- What values are important to the candidate? Honesty? Integrity? Trust?
- What are the candidate's expectations about this job?
- What kind of working conditions will the candidate find satisfactory?

Carefully interviewing and screening all job candidates is one definite way to prevent Negaholism from creeping into your organization. If you have the right people in the right positions and they like what they're doing, you should also have a successful team. After all, the success of a team depends largely on the success of its individual members.

There's a natural tendency when interviewing people to look for someone much like yourself. Subconsciously, we're more comfortable and at ease with people who have similar characteristics. So, if you're introspective, serious and well organized, you're more likely to hire someone with those same qualities than someone who's an extrovert, fun loving and creative. However, you need to realize that hiring a clone of yourself may not be the right thing for the organization. If this is a problem, ask a co-worker who's very different from you to also interview the candidate and then compare notes. Two perspectives are always better than one.

Another interviewing problem to avoid is the halo effect. This happens when you feel very comfortable or identify with a job candidate — maybe she has similar personality traits or she went to the same college that you did. As a result, you may "see" skills and abilities in this person that aren't really there. In other words, the candidate looks better to you than she really is.

No matter how hard you try to remain impartial during an interview, your personal agenda will have some influence over how you rate a candidate's skills, abilities, motivation and cultural fit. For instance, if you need a body to fill a position right now, your desperation could cloud your better judgment. Or, you might be more inclined to evaluate someone based on her potential rather than on her current status. So just because a job candidate's father was an outstanding car salesman doesn't mean the daughter will follow in his footsteps.

Interview Essentials

Each time you interview a job candidate keep these four guidelines in mind.

1. **Do 20 percent of the talking and 80 percent of the listening.** If you're the one doing most of the talking, then you're not learning what you should about the candidate. And that makes hiring the right person tougher than ever.
2. **Ask why more often than what.** This will force the candidate to tell you what motivated her to make certain job and career choices and changes. Carefully pay attention to determine if she's actually telling you the truth or simply telling you what she thinks you want to hear.

3. **Listen between the lines.** Be attuned to clues about the candidate's skills and abilities, motivation and cultural fit. Also listen for comments about what drives her, what her values are and what she expects and wants out of a job. Just be cautious about taking everything you hear at face value.

4. **Ask genuine, simple, direct, cut-to-the-chase types of questions.** This will help you connect with the job candidate. Don't play games. Most people appreciate an honest, straightforward interview. Here are three tips to help you.

   • **Take a genuine interest in the person.** The best way to do that is stop whatever you're doing and completely focus all of your attention on the candidate and the interview. Refuse to take phone calls or be interrupted. Look the person directly in the eye, really listen to her, take notes and convey through body language — such as nodding and leaning forward — that you understand what she's saying.

   • **Show a desire to make the person happy.** Do this regardless if you think the candidate will or won't get the job. Be courteous and curious. Ask lots of "why" questions that require answers about what motivates and makes the candidate happy.

   • **Demonstrate a willingness to be of service.** Despite the interview's outcome, answer all of the candidate's questions and concerns. However, don't give her false hopes. Making the right match between employee and job is more important than simply filling an open position. Help the candidate determine if your firm is a good match for her at the same time you're assessing her compatibility with the firm.

Exercise: The Whys Have It

Come up with three "why" questions that will help you best determine a job candidate's skills and abilities, motivation and cultural fit.

Skills and abilities

1. _____
2. _____
3. _____

Motivation

1. _____
2. _____
3. _____

Cultural fit

1. _____
2. _____
3. _____

Hopefully some of the questions you created sound like this:

- "Why did you choose this profession?
- "Why do you enjoy this type of work?"
- "Why were you drawn to that position?"
- "Why did you leave that job?
- "Why did you stay so long if you weren't happy?"

These types of questions and interviewing techniques are the best defense against allowing Negaholism and Negaholics to enter your workplace. Don't even let them in the front door, if you can help it.

Getting New Employees Off to a Good Start

What about those candidates who make the grade in terms of skills and abilities, motivation and cultural fit? Well, you hire them and welcome them into the organization with open arms. You also properly introduce and orient them to their new surroundings. Unfortunately, too many companies — large and small — overlook the importance of employee orientation. There's a lot more to it than handing out a benefits book and pointing out the locations of the restrooms and coffee pot.

Here's an example of what not to do. One large oil company hires very qualified and competent people. These new employees are typically introduced to their co-workers and shown around the office. They're assigned workstations and telephone extension numbers, told about the mission and goals of the company, and given an overview of the health care and profit-sharing plans. Then they're left to fend for themselves … often without a company organization chart or phone list. If they're lucky, within a year their bosses will conduct their performance reviews as they promised during the job interview. But that's only if they haven't managed to get lost in the shuffle somehow.

So what's wrong with this picture? Let me count the four ways:
1. You must orient your new employees effectively.
2. You must coach new employees into continued success.
3. You must mentor new employees with direction and certainty.
4. You must set expectations for new employees that are reasonable and attainable.

Orientation Essentials

Just what is orientation? It's a special program designed to answer new employees' questions before they ask them. In other words, it gives them all the pertinent information about the organization they need and want to know. An effective orientation program should include the following elements:

- An employee handbook that contains an overview of the organization and much of the following information
- Expectations the organization has for its employees (norms of behavior, dress code, work hours, flextime, etc.)
- The organization's mission statement
- The organization's values statement
- A history of the company
- Information about how the organization is owned, held or managed
- Names and information about officers and top management of the organization
- An organization chart
- Information about subsidiaries, divisions and departments
- Information about the organization's teams and how they're structured
- A list of acronyms for the organization
- Information about how new employees can participate in mentoring programs
- Information about how new employees can grow within the organization
- Information about where employees can go for support services (mailroom, document reproduction, conference planning, etc.)

An orientation program should be well thought out and clear. For example, you should never make assumptions about the knowledge level of a new employee. Many times organizations have their own languages and ways of doing things. What seems perfectly clear to a seasoned employee can be confusing to a new employee.

Take Maria's first day on a new job. Her boss asked her to take some new product specifications to "Repro" on the second floor so they could be copied. Maria assumed "Repro" was an employee who worked on the second floor. However, when she looked up the name in the employee directory and couldn't find it, she decided to go to the second floor and start searching for the right person. After 15 minutes of reading name plates on cubicles, Maria was stopped by another employee who noticed her panicked look. When Maria told the employee she was trying to locate someone named "Repro," the employee grinned and nodded. "You must be new," he observed. "Repro is what we call our document reproduction department. I'll take you there."

Many organizations' orientation programs have a detailed curriculum, handouts and a trainer to walk new employees through the labyrinth of information. Some are even offering these programs on their intranets, giving both new and longer-term employees easy computer access to all kinds of information about their organizations. These computer-based programs can be accessed and updated as needed.

If you really want new employees to get off to a great start in your organization, treat them the same way you'd treat your customers. (This applies to both internal and external customers.) Provide them with outstanding service and make their satisfaction your number one priority. Right now it may seem a bit silly, but this advice will pay dividends in the future.

I actually wrote my doctoral dissertation on the relationship between employee satisfaction and customer satisfaction. Believe it or not, they are parallel. My research indicates that the way managers treat their employees is directly reflected in the way those same employees treat their

"The customer's always right."

6

customers. Hence, the adage "Do unto your employees as you would have them do unto your customers!"

During your new employee orientation, demonstrate through your words and actions how you expect them to positively interact with one another. They'll be more inclined to deal with customers in a similar way. Also design and present your orientation program as if you were doing it for your very best customers. After all, your employees are the ambassadors of your organization. If they feel valued by management, they, in turn, will value their customers.

Making new employees feel welcome, wanted and valued is the first important step in preventing Negaholism from spreading throughout your organization.

Exercise: Getting Oriented

Create an orientation program for your organization if it doesn't already have one. Or if it does, decide how you would improve the existing one. State which elements you would include in your program.

Coaching Essentials

The next step you want to take with new employees is coaching. Through this process, managers support, encourage and direct their people so they can reach their highest potential. Just as a gymnastics coach works with an athlete to improve her skills on the balance beam, an organizational coach works with an employee to improve her skills on serving customer accounts. Just remember that a coach's job is never ending. Coaching is an ongoing process to ensure that your employees' potential is realized and even exceeded.

To be a successful coach follow these three steps:

1. **Create an agreement.** Make sure both coach and employee understand their roles, responsibilities, expectations and the length of their relationship.

Whether it's a written or a verbal agreement, it needs to be clear. While individual employees are usually assigned coaches, in team situations members should probably select a coach they all respect and one they feel will help them. The team also should agree on the style and method of coaching as well as when and how often coaching sessions will take place. Ideally, a coach should be identified as soon as possible after a team is formed.

6

2. **Establish clear goals.** In order to coach anyone or any team to pursue excellence, you must first set goals. These should be reasonable, realistic and attainable within the established timeframe. All people involved — coach and employee or coach and team members — need to agree on the goals. When discussing them, be sure to address these concerns:
   - Are the goals reasonable and realistic?
   - Are the goals attainable?
   - Can all timeframes be met?
   - Is there enough motivation to meet the goals?
   - Is there enough support to meet the goals?
   - Are there adequate resources to meet the goals?
3. **Set up sessions.** Coaching requires lots of time and effort. As a coach, you need to set aside blocks of time to meet with an employee or a team about any of the following topics:
   - Status reports — how everything's going and how everyone's doing
   - Achieving goals
   - Missing goals
   - Re-evaluating goals
   - Resetting timeframes for goals
   - Strategizing solutions

Here's how one team in a large conglomerate made coaching work for it. The team was comprised of very qualified, competent and intelligent people who seemed to agree on everything and who never argued or discussed anything. As a result, they didn't bother to set any goals or real action plans. However, that changed when team members selected a coach. He helped them choose a team leader, formulate team goals and establish due dates and individual accountability for each goal.

One of the coach's main jobs is to listen during team meetings and point out what members are overlooking, especially since they have a tendency to agree with one another automatically. When this happens, the coach typically interrupts and asks team members questions to get them back on track. For example, he might say, "Wait a minute, is this action consistent with our goal of reducing defects in our widget production?" A comment like this — also known as reflective feedback — forces team members to re-evaluate where they're headed.

When I act as a coach, I initially ask my client how things are going. Next I ask what progress is being made toward established goals and what obstacles are standing in the way. Then I brainstorm solutions with the client and finally ask what type of support I can lend. Before ending each coaching session, I make sure we've set definite dates for accomplishing specific and realistic tasks and also assigned the tasks to specific people.

First and foremost a coach is a supportive listener who empowers employees with encouragement, recognition and validation. Coaching is a widely accepted practice in healthy organizations that are committed to keeping out Negaholism.

Exercise: You Be the Coach

Think of an individual or team within your organization that could benefit from your coaching, then answer the following questions:

1. What kind of a coaching agreement would you create?

   _____

   _____

   _____

2. What would be your role and responsibilities?

   _____

   _____

   _____

3. What would be the roles and responsibilities of the employees?

   _____

   _____

   _____

4. How long would your agreement last?

   _____

   _____

   _____

5. What expectations would you have for your relationship?

   _____

   _____

   _____

6

6

6. What reasonable, realistic and attainable goals would you set?

_____

_____

_____

7. How would you motivate and support the employees so they could be assured of reaching their goals?

_____

_____

_____

8. How would you communicate to the employees how things are going and how everyone's doing?

_____

_____

_____

9. How would you handle situations such as missing goals, re-evaluating goals or resetting timeframes for achieving goals?

_____

_____

_____

10. How would you come up with solutions to problems that inevitably arise?

_____

_____

_____

6

Mentoring Essentials

Healthy organizations are also committed to mentoring as a way to prevent Negaholism from infecting their employees. Mentoring, which is often thought of as an alternative to coaching individuals, allows an employee to follow in your footsteps. A mentor is someone who has "been there, done that" and who gives the benefit of her knowledge, expertise and experience to a younger person or protégé. In some instances, a mentor may even help an entire team of individuals.

For example, a partner in a law firm may choose to take a promising young associate under her wing and teach her the ropes, so to speak. However, a mentor and protégé don't have to work for the same organization, but they typically share the same profession or at least have similar career interests. Mentor relationships like this are often less formal than coaching relationships. However, the objectives are very similar — to give another person guidance, direction and advice.

Use these criteria when establishing a mentoring program.

1. **Acknowledge the relationship.** A mentor must agree to help the other person. This can be done either through a formal or informal agreement. Often senior employees informally volunteer to be mentors for less experienced employees in their organizations. On the other hand, some companies formally identify key people, ask them to become mentors and then assign them to assist individuals or teams. As career planning and specific skill development have become more important to organizations so have organized mentoring programs. Whichever approach your organization takes, both mentors and protégés need a clear understanding of their relationships.

2. **Articulate your expectations.** Similarly, both parties need to clearly understand the expectations of

their relationship, such as how much time they'll spend together, where they'll meet, how they'll interact and what activities and tasks they'll work on. Using the two attorneys as an example, they might decide to meet for a two-hour lunch once a week. During that time, the pair could discuss the associate's assignments, with the senior partner giving advice on particular cases.

3. **Establish time frames.** Be specific about the mentoring commitment. When will the relationship start, how long will it last and when will it end? In some cases, these relationships last decades, with the mentor become a lifelong advisor and confidant to the protégé.

Exercise: You Be the Mentor

Think of an individual or team within your organization that could benefit from your mentoring then answer the following questions:

1. Would you prefer a formal or informal agreement?

   _____

   _____

   _____

2. How would you clearly define your relationship?

   _____

   _____

   _____

3. How much time would you spend together?

   _____

   _____

   _____

4. How often would you meet?

_____

_____

_____

5. Where would you meet?

_____

_____

_____

6. How will you interact?

_____

_____

_____

7. What kinds of tasks and activities would you work on?

_____

_____

_____

8. How long will the relationship last?

_____

_____

_____

9. When will the relationship begin or end?

_____

_____

_____

10. Do you think it should be a long-term relationship?

_____

_____

_____

6

6

> *"If you treat an individual as he is, he will stay as he is, but if you treat him as if he were what he ought to be and could be, then he will become what he ought to be and what he could be."*
>
> Johann Wolfgang von Goethe

Expectation Essentials

Nothing can cause Negaholism to set in faster than never meeting expectations. Employees become dejected and discouraged when they know they'll never be able to succeed at their jobs. Eventually, they'll give up and quit trying altogether.

For that reason organizations — as well as bosses, coaches and mentors — need to make sure expectations for their employees are reasonable and attainable. When an employee accomplishes her objectives, she builds self-esteem. When she fails to meet her objectives, she loses self-esteem. If it's your job to develop this employee, then you'll want to keep her in a building mode. Setting employees up for success is one of the greatest gifts you can give them. This involves knowing their limitations and helping them overcome them in a way that's positive and shows their progression.

For example, say one of your employees has a great deal of potential for being promoted within the organization. However, while she has great management and people skills, she lacks solid writing skills. Initially you encourage her to take a basic writing course at the local community college and even include the class as one of her personal objectives for the year. But you also decide to give her a series of job-related writing assignments. The first is a simple memo to co-workers about a team meeting. With direction and coaching from you, she successfully finishes it. Next you give her something a little more complex, such as a sample form letter that's sent to customers. Over the course of several months, you continue to raise the bar slightly with each new writing assignment, which she successfully completes. By the time the year's over, she's earned an "A" in her writing class and even penned a couple of detailed customer reports. Most importantly, she's gained a tremendous amount of self-esteem because the expectations set for her were reasonable and attainable.

All of the techniques discussed in this chapter underscore the need for employee feedback. This includes talking to your employees about where they are in terms of their development, how they're doing and what they need to work on more.

Feedback is one of the primary tools an organization uses to foster its growth. This is because employees don't always see themselves and their skills and abilities accurately. Their self-perception may be quite different from the way others see them. Feedback helps align their self-perceptions with reality. Whether you're a boss, coach or mentor, use feedback regularly. When it's offered in a positive and sensitive manner, feedback is yet another defense against Negaholism getting into your organization.

Questions for Personal Development

1. What is the major emphasis of this chapter?

   _____
   _____
   _____

2. What are the most important things you learned from this chapter?

   _____
   _____
   _____

3. How can you apply what you learned to your current job or your personal life?

   _____
   _____
   _____

6

4. How will you go about making these changes?

_____

_____

_____

5. How can you monitor improvement?

_____

_____

_____

6. Summarize the changes you expect to see in your co-workers and your organization one year from now.

_____

_____

_____

CHAPTER 7

How Your Negaholism Works Against You

If you suffer from Negaholism, you take the disease with you wherever you go. It not only impacts you but everyone around you including family members, friends and especially co-workers. In fact, your Negaholic tendencies may be at their worst on the job where you encounter daily stress, feel pulled in all directions and often become discouraged and frustrated by things beyond your control.

As I explained back in Chapter One, there are two sides to each of us: the "I can" side and the "I can't" side. They constantly battle each other. The "I can" side is confident, capable, strong and able to meet life's challenges and overcome them. In contrast, the "I can't" side lacks confidence and appears incapable and weak. It feels safe and comfortable with what's familiar, avoids taking risks and fears the unknown or anything that stretches us out of our comfort zones. Moreover, the "I can't" side imagines and prepares for the worst in order to stay safe. So the bigger the risks, the more forceful the "I can't side" becomes.

If you experience the "I can'ts" from time to time, consider yourself normal. It's when the "I can'ts" take over and you begin to believe in them that you're at risk.

> *"Life is a fatal complaint, an eminently contagious one."*
>
> Oliver Wendell Holmes

Just what does "at risk" mean? It means you talk yourself out of opportunities, you hold back when you could take a stand, and you disempower yourself. When you find yourself doing these things, you've exposed yourself to the Negaholic virus. In order to have a strong immune system to guard against Negaholism, you must have a healthy relationship with yourself. You must know and face the truth about yourself and be willing to share it with the world.

Case Study: Finding a Niche for Nina

A client named Nina hated her job as an executive secretary. It was clear that she didn't want to spend the rest of her life answering phones, typing letters and fetching coffee. I quickly pointed out that if being a secretary wasn't her passion, she should look elsewhere. I continued by asking Nina what she really enjoyed doing. She immediately answered that she loved to eat at elegant restaurants. I asked if there was anything else. She also mentioned shopping and speaking French, which she actually did quite well.

Her list left me at a loss. How could she possibly combine those three things into a new career? I wasn't sure about that, but I was sure about her passion for all of them. Nina absolutely sparkled when she spoke about any of the three.

Since I didn't have any obvious suggestions for her, I assigned Nina a research project — to find out how people make money eating, shopping and speaking French. She went to the library, compiled a list of contacts and came up with some questions to ask them.

Within a couple of weeks she called me and excitedly exclaimed, "I have a job!" Of course, I was delighted for her and asked for more details. "I'm working for an upscale department store that's planning a visit from several French designers. My job is to entertain the designers and the store's executive staff by taking them to elegant restaurants around the city. I'll also be translating French to English and English to French. Best of all, I get to eat wonderful food!"

C A S E S T U D Y

There are four important points to glean from Nina's story.

1. She admitted the truth to me and more importantly, herself.
2. She was completely honest with me and more importantly, herself.
3. She knew herself well.
4. She was willing to pursue and be supported in everything she really wanted.

Nina not only found a career she could excel at, but one she could truly enjoy. This is the key to avoiding Negaholism in your professional life. You need to understand your personal preferences and then match your individual skills and abilities to a career that you feel passionate about.

"The whole secret of a successful life is to find out what it is one's destiny to do, and then do it.

Henry Ford

7

Exercise: Know Thyself, Part I

Find a quiet place without distractions — a place where you can listen to your inner voice and recall what it's saying to you. Once you find that special place, complete the following phrases:

1. The times when I am the happiest are …

   _____

   _____

   _____

2. The most important thing to me is …

   _____

   _____

   _____

3. I'm really good at …

   _____

   _____

   _____

7

4. Things I really enjoy are …

_____

_____

_____

5. I'm passionate about …

_____

_____

_____

6. If I didn't have to be concerned about finances, I would …

_____

_____

_____

Completing these phrases is only the beginning. They will provide you with some direction on how to match yourself with your ideal job. And when you know yourself well, you receive many benefits. These include:

- **Getting your needs met.** If you can't identify what you want, then it's impossible for people to give it to you.
- **Creating conditions for satisfaction.** Satisfaction typically depends on getting your needs met.
- **Addressing boundary issues.** This involves setting reasonable limits for yourself.
- **Knowing your tolerances.** It's important to realize what you can take or accept as well as what you can't take or can't accept.
- **Operating at optimum performance.** When your needs are met and you feel satisfied, you're probably giving it your best effort and producing your best results.

Exercise: Know Thyself, Part II

Draw a line down the center of a blank piece of paper. Then intersect that line in the middle of the page with another straight line so you have four equal quadrants. In the upper-left quadrant, write the word "Strengths." In the upper-right quadrant, write the world "Weaknesses." Label the lower-left quadrant "Opportunities" and the lower-right quadrant "Threats." Now record everything you know and think about yourself in the most appropriate quadrant.

This kind of exercise is commonly known as a SWOT Analysis (S = Strengths, W = Weakness, O = Opportunities, T = Threats). It's a useful analytical tool because it encourages you to think about and lay out all aspects of yourself.

Once you've completed the exercise, ask a close and trusted family member or friend to provide you with feedback. If this person knows you well, he should be able to determine if something's missing. Furthermore, he can tell you if he agrees or disagrees with your analysis of yourself. His feedback will indicate how accurate your perceptions of yourself really are.

S = Strengths	W = Weaknesses
O = Opportunities	T = Threats

Exercise: The SELF Instrument

This exercise is based on a communications model. It will help you identify your preferences and how you relate to people and a job.

In answering questions one through 24, use the following scale. If you think the statement is not at all like you, mark number 1. If you think it is very much like you, mark 5.

1	2	3	4	5
Not at all	**Somewhat**	**Occasionally**	**Usually**	**Very much**

_____ 1. When in a group, I tend to speak and act as the representative of that group.

_____ 2. I am seldom quiet when I am with other people.

_____ 3. When faced with a leadership position, I tend to actively accept that role rather than diffuse it among others.

_____ 4. I would rather meet new people than read a good book.

_____ 5. Sometimes I ask more from my friends or family than they can accomplish.

_____ 6. I enjoy going out frequently

_____ 7. It's important to me that people follow the advice that I give them.

_____ 8. I like to entertain guests.

_____ 9. When I am in charge of a situation, I am comfortable assigning others to specific tasks.

_____ 10. I often go out of my way to meet new people.

_____ 11. In social settings, I find myself asking more questions of others than they ask of me.

_____ 12. I truly enjoy mixing in a crowd.

_____ 13. Other people usually think of me as being energetic.

_____ 14. I make friends very easily.

_____ 15. I am a verbal person.

_____ 16. I try to be supportive of my friends, no matter what they do.

7

_____ 17. If I see it's not going smoothly in a group, I usually take the lead and try to bring some structure to the situation.

_____ 18. I seldom find it hard to really enjoy myself at a lively party.

_____ 19. When in a leadership position, I like to clearly define my role and let followers know what is expected.

_____ 20. I consider myself to be good at small talk.

_____ 21. I am very good at persuading others to see things my way.

_____ 22. I can usually let myself go and have fun with friends.

_____ 23. I often find myself playing the role of leader and taking charge of the situation.

_____ 24. I do not prefer the simple, quiet life.

For questions 25-30, circle the letter representing your response.

25. You are in a conversation with more than one person. Someone makes a statement that you know is incorrect, but you are sure the others didn't catch it. Do you let the others know?
   A. Yes
   B. No

26. After a hard day's work I prefer to:
   A. Get together with a few friends and do something active.
   B. Relax at home and either watch TV or read.

27. When planning a social outing with a small group, I am most likely to:
   A. Be the first to suggest some plans and try to get the others to make a decision quickly.
   B. Make sure everyone has a say in the planning and go along with what the group decides.

28. You have just finished a three-month project for which you have sacrificed a great deal of your free time and energy. To celebrate, you are more likely to:
    A. Invite some of your friends over and throw a party.
    B. Spend a quiet, peaceful weekend doing whatever you wish, either by yourself or with a special friend.

29. If I feel that I am underpaid for my work, I'm most likely to:
    A. Confront the boss and demand a raise.
    B. Do nothing and hope the situation improves.

30. I think those around me see me as primarily:
    A. Gregarious and outgoing.
    B. Introspective and thoughtful.

Scoring the SELF Profile

Transfer your scores from questions 1 – 24 onto the grid below. For questions 25 – 30 give yourself a 5 for every A and a 1 for every B. Now add each column and record the total for each column as the directive and affiliative totals.

1. _____	2. _____
3. _____	4. _____
5. _____	6. _____
7. _____	8. _____
9. _____	10. _____
11. _____	12. _____
13. _____	14. _____
15. _____	16. _____
17. _____	18. _____
19. _____	20. _____
21. _____	22. _____
23. _____	24. _____
25. _____	26. _____
27. _____	28. _____
29. _____	30. _____

Directive Total _____ **Affiliative** _____

Using the scoring chart below, convert your Directive and Affiliative totals from the previous page. Then record your converted directive and affiliative scores (one through six) in the space provided just below the scoring chart.

If you scored from:	Give yourself a:
15-21	1
22-33	2
34-44	3
45-56	4
57-68	5
69-75	6

Converted Directive Score _____

Converted Affiliative Score _____

- On the graph at the top of the next page put a dot on the vertical (broken) line next to the number that is the same as your Converted Directive Score.
- Put a dot on the horizontal (dotted) line next to the number that is the same as your Converted Affiliative Score.
- Connect the two dots with a straight line.
- Now shade in the area of the triangle you've created.

Your SELF Profile Graph

6 High need to direct

5

Need people more

Affiliative 4 Need people less

6   5   4   3 3   2   1

Directive 3

2

1 Low need to direct

SELF Characteristics

Below are some characteristics that can be used to describe the tendencies of each dimension of SELF.

STRENGTHS

High

S
Persuasive
Risk-taker
Competitive
Pursues change
Confident
Socially skilled
Inspiring
Open
Direct
Outoing

E
Practical
Orderly
Very direct
Self-determined
Organized
Traditional
Goal-oriented
Dependable
Economical
Ambitious

Affiliative

High | **L** | **Low**

L
Team-oriented
Caring
Devoted
Enthusiastic
Helpful
Accessible
Trusting
Sensitive
Good listener
Good friend
Likes variety
Gregarious
Peacemaker

F
Exacting
Thorough
Factual
Reserved
Meticulous
Practical
Calm
Has high standards
Risk-avoider

Directive

Low

LIMITATIONS

High

S
Pushy
Intimidating
Overbearing
Restless
Impatient
Manipulative
Abrasive
Reactive
Dominating

E
Dogmatic
Stubborn
Rigid
Unapproachable
Distant
Critical
Insensitive

Affiliative

High | **L** | **Low**

L
Too other-oriented
Indecisive
Impractical
Vulnerable
Hesitant
Subjective

F
Slow to get things done
Perfectionistic
Withdrawn
Dull
Sullen
Shy
Passive

Directive

Low

7

The Importance of Self-Management

Ideally you want to know everything about yourself so that you can set yourself up for success. If you know you're outgoing, helpful and compassionate, then you should also realize you'd be more successful as a social worker than an accountant. Once you understand your personal preferences and match them with an appropriate job, the next step toward keeping Negaholism out of your world is effective self-management.

To effectively manage yourself remember these four important elements:

1. **Planning.** Create both short- and long-term goals and objectives for your career. Not only do these provide you with direction, but they also keep you on track and away from unhealthy procrastination patterns.

2. **Organization.** A place for everything and everything in its place. If you keep your desk and files well organized, you'll be able to immediately find them when you need them. Retrieving them becomes a simple task, not an overwhelming and time-consuming search.

3. **Prioritizing.** Weigh the importance of your projects, activities, meetings and daily tasks. Know what needs to come first, second, third and so on. Allocate your time and energy accordingly.

4. **Balance.** Make time for both work and play in your schedule. Spend quality time with family, friends and by yourself. Be sure to exercise, get enough rest, eat right and take care of yourself as well as others you may be responsible for. Too often, we put ourselves last on the priority list and run out of time just for us. As a result, we end up suffering the consequences: a bad case of Negaholism.

Managing your life is a lot like flying an airplane. You set a course, get sidetracked and then steer yourself back.

Adjusting the trim tabs every so often allows you to compensate for the wind and other factors that come along to throw you off course. It's critical that you constantly watch where you're headed.

Life requires the same diligence. Every January 1st, you come up with a list of New Year's resolutions to set a course for your life. But then demands at work, personal pressures and unanticipated emergencies send you off course periodically. Since it inevitably happens, try building some time to deal with these episodes into your regular schedule. You'll be glad you did.

If you stay on track for the most part, congratulate yourself. If you get off track, don't be too hard on yourself. Make the necessary adjustments to get back on course as soon as possible.

Exercise: Be Your Own Best Manager

Consider how you can improve your own self-management skills. Begin by answering the following questions:

1. Do you currently have short- and long-term goals and objectives for your career? If not, what kind of goals and objectives can you set?

    _____

    _____

    _____

2. Are your desk and files at work well organized? Can you quickly find things when you need them? If not, what steps can you take to become better organized?

    _____

    _____

    _____

3. Do you routinely prioritize your projects, activities, meetings and daily tasks? Do you know which are most important? How would prioritizing make your life easier?

_____

_____

_____

4. Do you make time for both work and play? Do you spend quality time with family members, friends and just by yourself? Do you exercise, get enough rest and eat right? Or do you always put yourself last on the priority list? How can you build time for yourself into your daily schedule?

_____

_____

_____

The Importance of Rewards

Another essential strategy of your anti-Negaholism campaign is rewards. When you do a good job, acknowledge it. Don't take yourself for granted. Give yourself a pat on the back or something special to celebrate your accomplishment and reinforce your positive behavior. A reward doesn't have to be anything extensive or expensive. It could be as simple as spending 15 minutes in a hot tub after a rigorous workout or stopping by a coffee shop for your favorite cup of cappuccino after giving a successful presentation to a client.

Let's face it — we all like and need attention. If you don't receive positive attention for behavior you want to reinforce, then you find a way to get it negatively. For example, how many times have you eaten a candy bar rather than an apple after exercising? You may have chosen the candy bar because despite all the workouts in the world you believe you'll never be able to lose weight.

"The sweetest of all sounds is praise."

Xenophon

Although Negative reinforcement like this is mostly subconscious, you can still do something about it. Each night before you go to bed, make a list of all the good things that happened to you — what you accomplished that day. Be sure to include "I" in every sentence, such as "I faxed George the revised project" or "I went to a step aerobics class." This is another way to pat yourself on the back, recognize the positives in your life and keep Negaholism at bay.

Exercise: Nightly Affirmations

Think about what you did yesterday. Try to list at least five positive things you accomplished. Be sure to include "I" in every sentence. Then continue this ritual every night before you go to bed.

What I Accomplished Today

1. _____
_____
_____

2. _____
_____
_____

3. _____
_____
_____

4. _____
_____
_____

5. _____
_____
_____

The Importance of Nurturing

The final preventive measure against Negaholism that you want to incorporate into your daily life is nurturing. Nurturing is an action you do to yourself for yourself, which demonstrates that you matter, that you care and that you are worthy of spending time, energy and, in some cases, money on.

Simply looking out your office window for a couple of minutes or getting a new pen and pad of paper from the supply area can be nurturing. Actions like these fill up your tank — they recharge you and restore your energy. Nurturing also can be spiritual, such as meditation, reflection or prayer. It's a way to say "I love you" to yourself, even if the rest of the world hasn't told you that lately.

10 Ways to Nip Negaholism in the Bud

During this chapter I've identified 10 key steps to keep Negaholism out of your life. Here they are:

1. **Reinforce the "I can" side of you.** Surround yourself with positive, supportive people who know that you're committed to strengthening the "I can" side and starving the "I can't" side.

2. **Be honest about your needs and wants.** Tell the truth about what you really need and what you really want. Don't fall into the trap of saying what you think others want to hear. Work on being honest with yourself too.

3. **Know yourself.** Know what works and what doesn't work for you. Be aware of your strengths and your weaknesses and communicate these to others so they know when to lend support.

4. **Discover your passion.** This is what makes your heart sing — what you love doing more than anything else. Even the very thought of this activity brings you pleasure and joy.

7

5. **Make plans.** Look ahead and decide what you want in the short-term, the long-term and the distant future.

6. **Prioritize.** Determine which tasks are most important, which ones are least important and which ones fall somewhere in the middle. Then do them in that order. If possible, complete tasks ahead of schedule.

7. **Get organized.** Don't waste more time than you have to retrieving information or finding things. Have a place for everything and put each item or file back immediately after you've finished using it. By doing this everything will be where it belongs.

8. **Keep your life in balance.** Remember the old saying "All work and no play makes Jack a dull boy"? This applies whether you're a Jack or a Jacqueline. Don't allow work, family or your other responsibilities and obligations to consume your life. Make time for you once in a while.

9. **Pat yourself on the back.** Acknowledge your accomplishments, reward yourself for a job well done and celebrate your successes. You deserve it!

10. **Nurture yourself.** In other words, be nice to yourself. Perform one simple act of kindness for yourself each day. Think of it this way: "A nurture a day keeps Negativity away."

All of these tips and techniques can keep you from falling victim to Negaholism. Just remember: the more change and stress you're exposed to and the higher your self-expectations are set, the more vulnerable you become to the Negaholic virus. Take these precautions, and most of all, take care of yourself.

Questions for Personal Development

1. What is the major emphasis of this chapter?

   _____
   _____
   _____

2. What are the most important things you learned from this chapter?

   _____
   _____
   _____

3. How can you apply what you learned to your current job or your personal life?

   _____
   _____
   _____

4. How will you go about making these changes?

   _____
   _____
   _____

5. How can you monitor improvement?

   _____
   _____
   _____

6. Summarize the changes you expect to see in yourself one year from now.

   _____
   _____
   _____

?

7

7

*C*HAPTER 8

Negaholism's Dirty Dozen

After researching Negaholism over three decades, I've determined that there are 12 different types of Corporate Negaholics. I call them the "Dirty Dozen." If you can learn to recognize these particular Negaholics at work, then you can take specific steps either to prevent the disease in others or overcome it yourself.

Let's get started by meeting the "Dirty Dozen" one by one and addressing what makes them the way they are. Like the Negaholics you met in Chapter Two, the Corporate "Dirty Dozen" are divided into four groups: Attitudinal, Behavioral, Mental and Verbal. Hopefully you'll come to understand each of them a little better and even empathize with them. This is at the heart of dealing with Negaholics.

When you judge someone in a Negative way, they become shunned just as lepers were in the past. People are reluctant to help a Negaholic because they're afraid it will rub off on them. Particularly in business, people avoid talking about Negaholism, and even if they admit it exists in their organization, they want to stay as far away from it as possible.

The truth is the closer you connect with a Negaholic, the more that person will feel your support and your

> *"One cool judgment is worth a thousand hasty councils. The thing to do is to supply light and not heat."*
>
> Woodrow Wilson

concern. Her "I can'ts" will begin to fade, and her "I cans" will become stronger.

For each of the "Dirty Dozen," I've listed several steps you can take to deal with that type of Negaholic in the workplace. Ideally, you want to build a productive working relationship with each one and even assist them in overcoming their addiction.

Attitudinal Corporate Negaholics

These are deeply dissatisfied people who believe they'll never truly enjoy work. Either they set such a high standard that it's impossible to live up to or they think they can never do enough, be good enough or have enough to please the internal demon that drives them. Despite all this, Attitudinal Corporate Negaholics are usually quite successful and appear normal on the outside. On the inside, however, they're tormented by their own inadequacies. Examples of this Negaholic are "The Workaholic Workhorse," "The Consummate Controller," "The Political Peacemaker," "The Perennial Expert," and "The Perennial Expert."

"The Workaholic Workhorse"

A blend of good news and bad news, "The Workaholic Workhorse" looks like the ideal employee on the outside. Warren, a single man in his late 30s, is devoted, loyal and willing to do whatever needs to be done. He arrives at work early, stays late and often comes in on weekends. His life is completely wrapped up in his work, and he takes a great sense of pride in this dedication, which borders on obsession. In effect, he's married to his job and appears to be fulfilled by it.

So why is Warren a bad influence on the organization? He sets a dangerous precedent. His co-workers tend to feel guilty if they're not working all the time too. They begin to spend more hours at the office, even though they may not be accomplishing any more. In fact, visibility comes to count more than productivity. This kind of behavior puts everyone in the organization at risk.

Here's how you can deal with "The Workaholic Workhorse."

- **Develop your assertiveness skills.** Refuse to be influenced by the precedent this person sets. Focus on your own work and doing a good job.

- **Identify tasks and timeframes.** Often the "Workaholic Workhorse" does work outside his own responsibilities and spends too much time on every task. Know exactly what your responsibilities include and set realistic timeframes for each one. For example, it's not necessary to spend an hour perfecting a three-paragraph memo to your co-workers.

- **Identify priorities.** "The Workaholic Workhorse" tends to make mountains out of molehills, placing too much emphasis on tasks that don't deserve the extra attention. Know what's important on your plate and focus your time and energy accordingly.

- **Put a limit on your work hours.** Don't fall into the trap of working 10 to 12-hour days. In most cases, you're not accomplishing a lot more than you would in eight or nine hours. Remember the law of diminishing returns: Your productivity hits a plateau and then begins to slide after so long. Better to quit at that point and start fresh the next day.

- **Sharpen your time management skills.** Learn to make the most of your time spent at work. Cut back on the time you spend talking with co-workers and milling around the coffee pot. If possible, take a time-management course that will help you maximize your productivity.

- **Lighten up on other people.** If you're a "Workaholic Workhorse," realize that not everyone shares your drive. Don't expect all of your co-workers to spend as much time at the office as you

8

do. Most of them have lives and responsibilities outside of work.

- **Get a life of your own.** There's more to life than work. That may seem incomprehensible to you if you're a "Workaholic Workhorse," but it's true. Start by joining something — whether it's a fitness club, a book group, a church or a volunteer effort. Find something else that gives you satisfaction.
- **Understand that OK is often good enough.** Many tasks don't require perfection or deserve the extra effort you put into them. They just aren't that important. As a "Workaholic Workhorse" you need to learn how to recognize these and deal with them appropriately.

"The Consummate Controller"

Charlie, a "Consummate Controller" needs to control everyone and everything within his domain. He wants to make sure things are done right, which means they're done his way. The good news is Charlie always produces a top quality product. However, the bad news is Charlie doesn't work well with others, especially those who are independent thinkers, creative or expressive. He isn't interested in their input or ideas because he knows exactly how everything should be: his way or the highway.

If you have a job that requires repetitive and exacting tasks, then Charlie's your man. If there's room for interpretation, then keep him as far away from it as possible. "Consummate Controllers" like Charlie stifle creativity, rob people of empowerment and eliminate risk-taking in an organization. Employees aren't encouraged or allowed to grow in this kind of environment. And when things stop growing, they stagnate or die.

8

To combat the "Consummate Controller," try these steps:

- **Create on-going accountability.** Don't allow the "Consummate Controller" to take charge. Let everyone have a hand in determining and taking responsibility for how things will get done. If necessary, make a chart showing who's responsible for each task or project.

- **Ask for small concessions.** Don't try to change a "Consummate Controller" all at once. Ask him to bend his rules slightly and one at a time. Eventually he may come to see that your way is better, but only if you take things slowly.

- **Suggest, don't demand.** When you approach "The Consummate Controller" about change, choose your words carefully. Suggest a different way of doing something, don't demand that he do it that way. Better yet, make him believe the change was his idea in the first place.

- **Focus on results, not methods.** "Consummate Controllers" are hung up on how things are done, not how well they're done. The bottom line of any organization is its productivity. Try to encourage him to be more results oriented, perhaps by offering incentives or rewards.

- **Keep him informed.** Often a "Consummate Controller" acts out of frustration because he feels left out of the loop. If he knows and understands what's going on in the organization, he'll be less likely to exert his control.

"The Political Peacemaker"

This Corporate Negaholic is one political animal. Polly has learned how to dress, what to say and whom she should associate with. In other words, she has the game figured out. Each day she plays a bigger-than-life chess match, in which she strategizes every move and plays to win. She's a keen observer, and she knows who has the power and who controls the purse strings. These are the people she aligns herself with. Polly relies on situational ethics, manipulates people for her own personal gain and says and does whatever she thinks will get her what she wants.

Unfortunately, Polly isn't trusted or liked by most of her co-workers. They see right through her, but they also fear her tactics. They know she's capable of using them at any time or for any reason. As a result, employees in the organization become paranoid — they don't feel safe to relax and just do their jobs. They're always on edge in this highly political environment.

So, how do you defeat or at least call a truce with a "Political Peacemaker"? Give these techniques a try.

- **Ask for specific information.** Know exactly what you're expected to do, how you're to do it and when it should be done. Don't leave any questions unanswered. The more you know and understand about a specific project or situation, the less likely "The Political Peacemaker" can disrupt it.

- **Get everything in writing.** This goes along with the previous point. If you feel the least bit uneasy about something, such as a project or a procedure, put it down on paper or ask someone else to do so. This is your proof in case "The Political Peacemaker" challenges you later.

- **Follow up religiously.** Don't leave any loose ends hanging. This is exactly the kind of ammunition against you that "The Political Peacemaker" constantly seeks.

- **Offer to do things yourself.** Don't rely on "The Political Peacemaker" to do the things she says she'll do. In fact, don't even ask for her help. Remember her words and actions are mostly for show.

- **Keep accurate records.** Again, this is your proof that you've done what you were expected to do. If you feel the need, also keep track of what "The Political Peacemaker" has promised but failed to deliver. Your records could come in handy down the road.

"The Perennial Expert"

You probably referred to this kind of Corporate Negaholic as "Miss Know It All" in grade school. Now all grown up, she's become "The Perennial Expert."

Take Elaine, for instance. She's overly impressed with her own importance in the organization. She always assumes the position of expert on any issue, whether she actually knows anything about it or not. Furthermore, she always offers her advice and her solutions, whether they're sought or not. She seldom asks questions; she has all the answers instead.

With an Elaine in their midst, other employees don't feel safe to learn, grow, ask questions or know anything on their own. They don't feel empowered. They also don't work well in team situations because Elaine inevitably takes charge and runs the show. Remember, there's isn't an "I" in team.

If you want to co-exist with a "Perennial Expert" like Elaine, follow these guidelines:

- **Know your facts and figures.** Don't automatically allow "The Perennial Expert" to serve as the expert every time. Keep yourself informed. You may even discover that "The Perennial Expert" makes a mistake once in a while. If that happens, challenge her. Let her know she's not the only expert around.

- **Let her take the credit.** Even if you came up with the best solution to a problem, let "The Perennial Expert" have all the glory. She'd probably take it from you one way or the other anyway. Be heartened by the fact that most people see through her attempts to steal the show. In the long run, you'll gain extra points for being the silent hero.

- **Ask questions.** This shows you're interested, involved and focused on what's ahead. Unfortunately, "The Perennial Expert" may offer all the answers, whether she's qualified or not.
- **Agree ... and then ask another question.** Be persistent. Don't let "The Perennial Expert" take complete control. Also avoid arguing with her. If you immediately agree with her, she may stop talking long enough for you to make a point.

The Chronic Cynic

Do you often hear the comments "It can't happen" or "No way, it's just not possible" to almost every request you make? Meet John, a "Chronic Cynic" who approaches all tasks with a negative can't-do attitude. He eagerly awaits the opportunity to say that something simply can't be done.

John not only makes arguments supporting his own limitations, but makes arguments regarding the limitations of others as well. He won't be able to do what you need, and claims that others won't be able to, either. John is simply adamant that things cannot and will not work out. As far as he's concerned, happy endings are not a possibility, and any suggestion you make to the contrary is treated with contempt.

How does behavior associated with Chronic Cynic Negaholism become contagious in an organization? This "we can't" attitude is a virus that takes hold, takes control, and spreads like an epidemic throughout a company.

What you can do about "The Chronic Cynic":

- **Respond to sarcasm. Ignore or deflect sarcastic comments.** Don't allow sarcasm to get you off track or lose sight of your goal. Ask "The Chronic Cynic" what he needs to complete tasks associated with your request.
- **Challenge negatives.** Put a positive angle on negative predictions. Demonstrate your belief that a positive outcome is possible.

- **Ask for specifics.** Ask what needs to be done, when it needs to be done, and by whom. This will help break a task down into manageable parts. This is especially helpful if you're "The Chronic Cynic."
- **Encourage "What if … "** Find out what "The Chronic Cynic" needs to succeed and then find ways to provide him with that support. Develop possible scenarios for success. In this way, you can enable "The Chronic Cynic" to see other possibilities.
- **Give ground-level action steps.** If "The Chronic Cynic" still resists the possibility of a successful outcome, show him what first steps can be taken to get a project off the ground and on its way. Rather than looking to the end result, help devise the initial means of getting there.
- **Set him or her up to succeed.** Work out a time frame and develop a course of action that will guarantee success. Provide needed support. Once the task is completed, "The Chronic Cynic" will have experienced the achievement of a positive outcome. Future successes will seem possible. If he succeeds once, he can succeed again.

Exercise: Analyzing Attitudinal Corporate Negaholics

Now that you've met the four kinds of Attitudinal Corporate Negaholics, answer the following questions:

1. Which telltale signs of "The Workaholic Workhorse" do you see in yourself or your co-workers? What drives these actions? What steps will you take to deal with these Negaholic tendencies?

_____

_____

_____

2. Which telltale signs of "The Consummate Controller" do you see in yourself or your co-workers? What drives these actions? What steps will you take to deal with these Negaholic tendencies?

_____

_____

_____

3. Which telltale signs of "The Political Peacemaker" do you see in yourself or your co-workers? What drives these actions? What steps will you take to deal with these Negaholic tendencies?

_____

_____

_____

4. Which telltale signs of "The Perennial Expert" do you see in yourself or your co-workers? What drives these actions? What steps will you take to deal with these Negaholic tendencies?

_____

_____

_____

5. Which telltale signs of "The Chronic Cynic" do you see in yourself or your co-workers? What drives these actions? What steps will you take to deal with these Negaholic tendencies?

_____

_____

_____

8

Behavioral Corporate Negaholics

Like their colleagues with Attitudinal Negaholism, Corporate Behavioral Negaholics are often successful, but they suffer from at least one behavior that keeps them from realizing all of their objectives. Sometimes they succeed in spite of themselves. However, in most cases, they're slightly off the mark due to some element of self-sabotage.

Caught in this discrepancy between their ideas and their actions, they constantly try but can't seem to break out of their destructive behavioral patterns. These patterns include compulsion about work, isolation, smoking, excessive drinking, overeating, illegal drug usage, and overindulgence in gossip, time wasting or playing practical jokes on co-workers. Among the Behavioral Corporate Negaholics are "The Blatant Back-Stabber," "The Status Quo Sustainer" and "The Solitary Succeeder."

"The Blatant Back-Stabber"

Barbara's specialty is saying the wrong thing to the wrong person at the wrong time. And it gets worse. She's completely oblivious to the fact that her co-workers take offense at her cattiness, pettiness, put-downs and covert hostility. Barbara will say one thing to your face and another behind your back five minutes later.

Whatever you do, don't trust this kind of Negaholic. People like Barbara will use anything you say or do against you later. In general, watch out because she's trouble. When she's around, co-workers are mistrustful and uneasy. They spend so much time watching their backs and covering their tracks that the organization's productivity suffers.

Here's what you can do to get back at "The Blatant Back-Stabber."

- **Grill the messenger.** Find out exactly what "The Blatant Back-Stabber" said about you behind your back. Ask lots of questions so you get the story straight.

- **Prepare your case.** Decide how you'll tell your side of the story. Be able to back up your claims with any concrete evidence, if it exists.
- **Confront her.** Don't get angry; remain calm and in control. Tell her you know what she's been saying about you and that you don't appreciate it. It's critical not to lose your cool here.
- **Challenge and discredit erroneous "facts."** Set the record straight by finally telling your side of the story. Don't allow her lies to be perceived as the truth. Address every inaccuracy calmly and rationally.
- **Shift the focus from you to her.** Don't become her victim. Defend yourself and then go on the offensive. Point out how she's discredited you.

"The Status Quo Sustainer"

Also known as the peacemaker, this Corporate Negaholic will go to great lengths to deny or avoid admitting that anything is ever wrong. Someone like Stan is a classic non-confrontationalist. He doesn't like friction; he doesn't like change; he doesn't rock the boat. Instead he maintains the status quo at all costs. Stan is more concerned about peace and harmony than about truth, honesty, problems, solutions or results.

When there are too many Stans in an organization, there is also little or no innovation and natural evolution in the organization. Employees become afraid of change. They get stuck in a rut and so does the organization. To kick start Stan and other "Status Quo Sustainers" like him, try these steps:

- **Ask for small concessions.** You'll never change a "Status Quo Sustainer" overnight, so go for little victories. For example, even if you think the entire order fulfillment process needs overhauling, start with something simple like updating the order forms first. Once he gets used to this small change, suggest another one.

- **Be persistent and patient.** Don't give up, but don't go for a home run either. Think in terms of base hits, and don't throw him any curve balls. The only way you'll ever change a "Status Quo Sustainer's" behavior is slowly, methodically and predictably.
- **Use the "If ... then" approach.** If the "Status Quo Sustainer" still resists your suggestion, try logic. Again, slowly and methodically explain how your idea will change things for the better. For example, "If we update and streamline our order forms, then we won't spend so much time filling them out. That will save us several minutes of work time every day."
- **Take only calculated risks.** Carefully consider what you're asking "The Status Quo Sustainer" to do. Suggest changes that put him at little risk and that he'll be more apt to accept. If you go too far out on a limb, he'll never be willing to listen to you again.

"The Solitary Succeeder"

This Corporate Negaholic is a loner. Let's use Solomon as an example. He's extremely capable of managing tasks and projects on his own, but he can't function on a team. While he knows he can count on himself, he doesn't trust others and refuses to rely on them to get the job done. As a result, his scope is limited to what he can accomplish by himself.

In fairness, some of Solomon's solitary feats are truly Herculean. His colleagues actually admire and respect his abilities and discipline, but they also are suspect of his desire for isolation. What Solomon doesn't realize is that he's restricting himself and his future by not being a team player. He's giving up opportunities to grow, learn and move up in the organization — all because he's afraid of mistakes and imperfections. He wants to play it safe and play it alone.

Here's how you can get "The Solitary Succeeder to open up a bit.

8

8

- **Keep your word when dealing with him.** Because "The Solitary Succeeder" is distrustful of others, make sure you live up to your promises. Go out of your way to let him know that you're someone he can count on. After several positive interactions like this, he may actually come to trust you.
- **Negotiate pieces of the job.** While "The Solitary Succeeder" won't want to give up his control over an entire project, he might be persuaded to let you take on parts of it. However, this will only happen if you earn his trust first.
- **Ask him to teach you.** As I said before, a "Solitary Succeeder" is very good at certain things, such as research and writing reports. Pick an area where he excels and you need some work, then ask for his help. He'll probably be flattered you asked. Plus it will provide him with a positive experience of working with another person.
- **Promote a team spirit.** Whenever "The Solitary Succeeder" plays a part — no matter how small — in a team project, celebrate! Recognize and reward his efforts in a big way. Allow him to see that being part of a team can be an enjoyable experience.

Exercise: Analyzing Behavioral Corporate Negaholics

Now that you've met the three kinds of Behavioral Corporate Negaholics, answer the following questions:

1. Which telltale signs of "The Blatant Back-Stabber" do you see in yourself or your co-workers? What drives these actions? What steps will you take to deal with these Negaholic tendencies?

   _____

   _____

   _____

2. Which telltale signs of "The Status Quo Sustainer" do you see in yourself or your co-workers? What drives these actions? What steps will you take to deal with these Negaholic tendencies?

   _____

   _____

   _____

3. Which telltale signs of "The Solitary Succeeder" do you see in yourself or your co-workers? What drives these actions? What steps will you take to deal with these Negaholic tendencies?

   _____

   _____

   _____

Mental Corporate Negaholics

These Negaholics constantly beat up on themselves, typically for mistakes they've made in the past as well as for ones they feel certain they'll make again in the future. When they screw up something, they can't let it go and move on. Instead they ruthlessly flog themselves through self-criticism, invalidation, harsh judgements and self-inflicted mental abuse. Worst of all, they allow these Negative thoughts to run their lives and drive their behavior. "The

Morose Melancholic" and "The Walking Wounded" are both examples of Mental Corporate Negaholics.

"The Morose Melancholic"

Melody, a "Morose Melancholic," always sings a sad tune. You'll hear her say things like:

- "It hasn't worked, it doesn't work, and it never will work."
- "Life is tough. Unfortunately, you have to work to pay the bills."
- "You're never going to like your job, so just do any old thing, then take the money and run."
- "There's no way out, you're trapped. So stop fighting it and accept the fact that it's going to be like this for the rest of your life."

Sounds like chronic depression, doesn't it? Well, it's close. While depression is a condition, this is the way a "Morose Melancholic" perceives life — sad, full of resentfulness, hopeless, helpless and unable to change herself, her situation or her behavior.

At the office, Melody simply punches in and punches out. She does her job adequately and goes home. For her work is drudgery — something to be tolerated from paycheck to paycheck. Melody sees her life as going nowhere, with only dead ends ahead of her. She'd like to change, maybe even venture out and start her own business, but she's too scared. So she stays where she is — caught between what she wants and what she tells herself she can't have. As a result, she feels absolutely paralyzed and chronically unhappy.

The real trouble with a "Morose Melancholic" like Melody is that her Negativity easily rubs off on others. She can convince co-workers that the worst is bound to happen, affecting morale and snuffing out any positive change in the organization.

"Melancholy is the pleasure of being sad."

Victor Hugo

8

To lessen a "Morose Melancholic's" impact on the organization follow these suggestions:

- **Repeat and exaggerate what she says.** Hopefully this will convince her how silly and outrageous most of her comments are. They may sound absolutely absurd to her when they come from someone else.

- **Refuse to sink to her level.** Don't allow yourself to get sucked into a "Morose Melancholic's" Negaholism. Stay above it ... where you can still breathe.

- **Turn Negatives into positives.** When the "Morose Melancholic" says something Negative, try to turn it into something positive. That sounds like a tall order, and it is. But be creative and use your imagination. For example, if she says "Accept the fact that it's going to be like this for the rest of your life," then come back with "Well, think of the alternative — death!"

- **Ignore her when you have to.** A "Morose Melancholic" can really grate on your nerves. So, if her comments are more than you can take, tune her out.

- **Show compassion for her condition.** Don't make fun of "The Morose Melancholic." Her beliefs are very real to her, although they may seem ridiculous to you. Realize she feels absolutely helpless to change her condition.

"The Walking Wounded"

A "Walking Wounded" Negaholic like Walter lives a mouse-like existence. He keeps a low profile at work, tries not to make waves, stays out of the way and behaves himself all the time. It's easy to completely overlook Walter and that's the way he prefers it.

The "Walking Wounded" don't want to be noticed due to any one of the following reasons: an embarrassing past

8

incident, a physical handicap, a mental impairment, an emotional trauma, insecurity, fear of people or just plain old chronic shyness. They quietly do their jobs without attracting attention and without showing any ambition for getting more out of life.

For the most part, people like Walter don't cause trouble, but they can drain the energy out of an organization. Here's what you can do to add a little more life to "The Walking Wounded."

- **Require performance standards.** Make sure "The Walking Wounded" understands what's required of him and then hold him accountable. If you don't, he'll slip farther and farther into the background. You might forget about him altogether.

- **Give him lots of encouragement.** Praise him, reward him and pat him on the back when he does a good job. Maybe he'll be enticed to do more next time. Better yet, he may be willing to step a little further out of his shell.

- **Practice simple acts of kindness.** Whenever possible, be kind to "The Walking Wounded." Ask him to join you for a cup of coffee at break time or offer to take his customer calls if he's out sick.

- **Withhold sympathy, but extend compassion.** "The Walking Wounded" doesn't want your pity. In fact, he'd rather that you not notice him at all. However, he does deserve your understanding, and you should be sensitive to his condition.

- **Refuse to take on his issue.** Unless you're a psychiatrist, psychologist or highly trained counselor, don't go too far in attempting to help a "Walking Wounded." His condition warrants professional help. Offer your support, but nothing more.

- **Encourage counseling.** If you feel comfortable talking with "The Walking Wounded," you might suggest that he seek the help of a mental health

8

professional. However, don't push the issue. You may end up doing more harm than good.

Exercise: Analyzing Mental Corporate Negaholics

Now that you've met the two kinds of Mental Corporate Negaholics, answer the following questions:

1. Which telltale signs of "The Morose Melancholic" do you see in yourself or your co-workers? What drives these actions? What steps will you take to deal with these Negaholic tendencies?

_____

_____

_____

2. Which telltale signs of "The Walking Wounded" do you see in yourself or your co-workers? What drives these actions? What steps will you take to deal with these Negaholic tendencies?

_____

_____

_____

Verbal Corporate Negaholics

These people will either drive you crazy or force your own latent Negaholism to rise to the surface. So the best advice is to stay as far away from them as you can. They constantly focus on the Negative and the worst things that can possibly happen. If you don't maintain your sense of humor around them, you'll quickly become depressed. There are two types of Corporate Verbal Negaholics to watch out for: "The Garrulous Gossip" and "The Resigned Apathetic."

"The Garrulous Gossip"

The exact opposite of "The Walking Wounded," Ginger craves constant attention. The non-stop chatter of this

8

"Garrulous Gossip" drives everyone at work crazy. She never quits spreading the latest round of office gossip and sometimes allows confidential information to indiscriminately leak out.

Despite these shortcomings, Ginger is helpful, capable, competent and efficient. It's her nervousness and insecurity that keep her mouth moving all the time. Her secret bits of office information make her feel incredibly intelligent. In fact, she sometimes thinks she should be heading up the organization and doesn't hesitate to let you know that.

Too many Gingers tend to erode the credibility of an organization. Employees become too distracted with gossip, rumors and innuendo, and they forget to focus on the real work at hand. If you need to confront a "Garrulous Gossip," ask her these questions or respond with these comments:

- **"Where did you hear this?"** Force "The Garrulous Gossip" to name the source. In many instances, she won't have one. It's just her over-active imagination at work.
- **"How do you know it's true?"** Again you're questioning her credibility and how she obtained the information. As a result, she may be less inclined to tell the same thing to the next person she sees.
- **"I'm really surprised to hear that!"** This shows you have doubts about the validity of her statement. You've put "The Garrulous Gossip" in the position of having to defend herself, which she may or may not be able to do.
- **"Will you go with me to talk to this person?"** Now you've really backed her into a corner. She either has to admit she's lying or rush to reclaim her credibility.
- **"Can I use your name?"** This also puts "The Garrulous Gossip" on the spot. If her statement isn't true, she needs to be ready to face the consequences.
- **"Let's clear up this matter right now."** You've reached the point of no return. Either way "The

Garrulous Gossip" loses. If she lied, she may be fired or suspended. And even if she was telling the truth, she may still be disciplined or reprimanded for not minding her own business.

"The Resigned Apathetic"

"Nothing is ever going to change around here, so why bother?" That's a comment you'll often hear coming from Reginald, "The Resigned Apathetic." He lives by the motto: "If it ain't broke, don't fix it." Therefore, he rarely gets excited or enthusiastic about anything, nor does he get particularly angry or upset. In fact, his reaction to just about everything is neutral.

It's important not to let Reginald's apathy and resignation spread to other employees or other parts of the organization. Here's what you can do to make sure that doesn't happen.

- **Be a coach, not a crutch.** Don't let yourself become an easy ear for Reginald's comments. If he starts to sound a little Negative, stop him. Ask him why change won't make a difference. Force him to answer his own complaints.
- **Solicit his participation.** Don't allow your "Resigned Apathetic" to stand on the sidelines another minute. Get him involved now.
- **Listen actively.** Look for the underlying message in his comments. Try to understand why he's apathetic and resigned to things the way they are.
- **Challenge him with humor.** If you can get "The Resigned Apathetic" to laugh or even smile, you've made great strides. Humor is a wonderful way to open people up.
- **Give him more than applause — give him a standing ovation.** Since "The Resigned Apathetic" doesn't get too excited or enthused about anything, you've got to make up for his lack of response. Over-reward and over-celebrate his

8

accomplishments. Toot his horn shamelessly. Make him feel like he's the greatest thing since sliced bread. Maybe you'll get a rise out of him then.

Exercise: Analyzing Verbal Corporate Negaholics

Now that you've met the two kinds of Verbal Corporate Negaholics, answer the following questions:

1. Which telltale signs of "The Garrulous Gossip" do you see in yourself or your co-workers? What drives these actions? What steps will you take to deal with these Negaholic tendencies?

   _____

   _____

   _____

2. Which telltale signs of "The Resigned Apathetic" do you see in yourself or your co-workers? What drives these actions? What steps will you take to deal with these Negaholic tendencies?

   _____

   _____

   _____

Questions for Personal Development

1. What is the major emphasis of this chapter?

   _____

   _____

   _____

2. What are the most important things you learned from this chapter?

   _____

   _____

   _____

3. How can you apply what you learned to your current job or your personal life?

   _____

   _____

   _____

4. How will you go about making these changes?

   _____

   _____

   _____

5. How can you monitor improvement?

   _____

   _____

   _____

6. Summarize the changes you expect to see in yourself and your co-workers one year from now.

   _____

   _____

   _____

8

CHAPTER 9

Why Negaholism Sets In

Now that you've met the "Dirty Dozen," you may wonder how they ever got that way. Corporate Negaholism doesn't miraculously appear overnight. It slowly builds over weeks, months and years based on an individual's personality traits, attitudes and behaviors, coupled with his experiences both at work and at home.

Negaholic Hot Buttons

Many of these Negaholic issues start on a personal level but bleed over into a Negaholic's professional life. There are 10 of these issues:

1. **Abandonment.** Fear of being left behind plagues many people who were raised in dysfunctional homes. They feel left out, unimportant or simply forgotten. Work activities that include change, such as promotions, layoffs, acquisitions, mergers, buy-outs and even award banquets, can seriously affect a Negaholic employee who fears abandonment.

2. **Control.** People from dysfunctional homes often see control as a major issue in their lives. It's typically because they've either been dominated by overly-strict parents or allowed to

run wild with no parental supervision. As a result, these Negaholics either feel an overwhelming need to control others or they feel out of control and continually search for stability.

3. **Boundaries.** This involves the inability to say no and set reasonable limits. People who grow up in dysfunctional homes may not be able to differentiate among their needs and those of other people and other situations. On the job, this inability to say no and set limits translates into workaholism.

4. **Denial.** Denying or avoiding reality is a learned behavior for those from dysfunctional families. In a work environment, it results in running from the truth or internalizing issues rather than confronting them.

5. **Independence/Dependence.** Being trapped in a dysfunctional home can give off mixed messages: the need for both independence and dependence on the job. For example, one moment a Negaholic might say "Get away from me. I can do it myself." The next minute, the message is "Come here. I need for you to help me."

6. **Responsibility/Irresponsibility.** Either an over-developed sense of responsibility or a complete lack of it is typically found in Negaholic personalities. If they grew up in an unpredictable and unstable environment, they become overly responsible adults. However, if they grew up in a strict and uncompromising environment, they may become totally irresponsible adults.

7. **The need to be liked.** Since rejection and abuse were likely a part of their dysfunctional past, Negaholics will do anything to avoid more of the same. Having people like them and feeling loved are their top priorities. They avoid confrontation at all costs — either through compromise or by clamming up.

8. **Authority.** There may be mixed messages when it comes to authority too. One minute Negaholics will cry out for structure and limits, while the next they'll rebel against any authority figures. This latter tendency may stem from authority figures from their childhood who were unreliable and unpredictable.

9. **The need for excitement, drama and chaos.** Over-stimulating events — such as confrontations, crises, emergencies, traumas and calamities — are a way of life in a dysfunctional families. In later life, Negaholics often search for that adrenaline rush that gives them the feeling of being alive and kicking.

10. **Loyalties.** People raised in dysfunctional homes display extreme loyalty. It usually comes from dealing with a dysfunctional parent and later is transferred to an unhealthy supervisor or work situation. Negaholics' extreme loyalty often supersedes their own interests and well-being.

In addition to these 10 Negaholic issues, there are five main reasons why people become Corporate Negaholics.

1. Their jobs don't match their interests and personalities.
2. They have low self-esteem.
3. They feel stressed and overwhelmed.
4. They act out negatively to get attention.
5. They harbor hurts and resentments from the past.

Let's more closely examine each of these five reasons and see what steps can be taken to lessen their effects.

Mismatched People and Positions

When an employee doesn't fit his job, he makes himself and everyone around him miserable. He whines, he pouts, he complains, and he doesn't do a good job, leaving his co-workers to take up the slack.

So how did this happen? Usually for one of two reasons. First, he desperately needed a job so he took the only one that was available. Or second, he originally fit the position, but now he's outgrown it and no one's noticed.

Whichever the case, he doesn't have the communication skills or the assertiveness to say he needs a change. He's afraid he'll lose his job altogether. Instead of taking action, he stays where he is and suffers.

Case Study: A Better Match for Malcolm

When Malcolm graduated from college, he began interviewing for jobs. His friend Ashley told him about an opening at her insurance company. Ashley loved her job because the work was relatively easy, the pay and benefits were good, and it was close to home, which cut down on commuting time. It sounded good to Malcolm, too. He got an interview and was soon offered a job, which he accepted.

Three years have now passed. Malcolm still finds himself in the same position. Unfortunately, he's accumulated thousands of dollars in credit card debt, gotten behind on paying his student loan and leased a new car. Needless to say, he's living from paycheck to paycheck. He's lost all the enthusiasm he had in college as well as a sense of direction. He feels trapped in his job. He isn't exactly unhappy, but he isn't motivated or productive either.

In order for Malcolm to regain his enthusiasm and become a focused and positive employee again, he needs to take a step back and find out who he is and what he wants. This can be difficult to do in the midst of dozens of other daily activities. Malcolm's boss could help by regularly appraising his performance and by giving him meaningful and relevant feedback about his attitude and productivity. Armed with this feedback, Malcolm would be motivated and better prepared to find a new position or profession that more closely matches his skills, abilities and preferences. Everyone would be happier — Malcolm, his boss and his co-workers.

CASE STUDY

9

Exercise: The Match Game

After reading this section, answer the following questions:

1. Is your current job a good fit for your skills, abilities and personal preferences?

   _____

   _____

   _____

2. If not, why did you take the job?

   _____

   _____

   _____

3. Why do you remain in the job?

   _____

   _____

   _____

4. What steps can you take to rediscover your enthusiasm and career direction? How might others help you?

   _____

   _____

   _____

5. Do you have co-workers who are trapped in jobs that don't fit their skills, abilities and personal preferences?

   _____

   _____

   _____

6. Why did they take their jobs?

   _____

   _____

   _____

7. Why do they remain in their jobs?

_____

_____

_____

8. What steps could they take to rediscover their enthusiasm and career direction? How might you help?

_____

_____

_____

Low Self-Esteem

Employees with low self-esteem feel unable, untrained, uneducated, ill equipped or just plain unworthy to do their jobs. And guess, what? Their jobs don't get done most of the time. When they do, they're not done correctly or adequately. The low self-esteem becomes a self-fulfilling prophesy for these employees. Because they believe they can't, they can't. Co-workers are forced to do their work for them or, at the very least, cover their tracks so they don't get fired.

Left to their own devices, employees suffering from low self-esteem talk themselves out of every opportunity that comes their way. The only thing that will help them is working closely with a boss, coach or mentor who can begin to turn their attitudes around. Through confidence and skill building, continuing education and training, employees with low self-esteem can learn new behaviors and competencies.

Case Study: Louisa's Low Self-Esteem

Louisa did a good job as a customer service representative for a telemarketing company, and eventually her boss decided to promote her to supervisor. Initially, she was excited about the promotion until she realized she didn't have any supervisory skills. After all, she'd never been in charge or managed other people.

9

C A S E   S T U D Y

After accepting the job, Louisa was too embarrassed to admit her shortcomings. She tried to mask her feelings of incompetence by joking around with members of her team and acting more like a co-worker than a team leader. Members lost all respect for Louisa's authority, and they began to take advantage of her. Over time, the team's performance dipped dramatically, and Louisa found herself being reprimanded. Once she started a downward spiral, she brought the entire team with her.

After offering her the promotion, Louisa's boss should have sent her to a course for newly appointed supervisors and also encouraged her to enroll in a leadership training program. It was obvious she needed more than on-the-job training. Louisa's Negative experience as a supervisor lowered her self-esteem. Unfortunately, this could have been avoided with the proper training and support from her own supervisor.

Exercise: Evaluating Self-Esteem

After reading this section, answer the following questions:

1. Do you suffer from low self-esteem and feel unable, untrained, uneducated, ill equipped or just plain unworthy to do your job?

   _____

   _____

   _____

2. What are the sources of these feelings?

   _____

   _____

   _____

C A S E   S T U D Y

9

3. What kinds of personal support will help you overcome your feelings of low-self esteem?

_____
_____
_____

4. What kinds of training will help you overcome your feelings of low self-esteem?

_____
_____
_____

5. Do you know co-workers who suffer from low self-esteem and feel unable, untrained, uneducated, ill equipped or just plain unworthy to do their jobs?

_____
_____
_____

6. What are the sources of their feelings?

_____
_____
_____

7. What kinds of personal support will help them overcome their feelings of low self-esteem?

_____
_____
_____

8. What kinds of training will help them overcome their feelings of low self-esteem?

_____
_____
_____

Feeling Stressed and Overwhelmed

Back in Chapter Four, I discussed how change exacerbates stress, which, in turn, drives people to feel overwhelmed. In the workplace, stress is often caused by technological change. It seems we just get used to a new computer or a new data entry system and another one comes along to take its place.

When an employee feels stressed and overwhelmed by change, the "I can'ts" totally take over, dictating his perceptions of reality. He believes he can't do anything. "I can't get out of bed; I can't take a shower; I can't go to work." Of course, this isn't quite true. But since he believes it, it's become a reality for him.

Most stressed and overwhelmed employees try to conceal rather than communicate their "I can'ts." They're afraid to acknowledge their self-doubts and fears, especially if their organizations tend to look down on people who do this. So instead, they internalize their "I can't" feelings and insufficiencies even more.

Case Study: Stressed-Out Suzie

For 25 years Suzie worked on the line in the manufacturing division of a large corporation. When the top brass decided to close the plant where Suzie worked, she worried if she'd lose her job, her pension and her security after all those years. Fortunately, because of her seniority, Suzie was reassigned to work as a customer service representative in one of the corporation's local telemarketing centers. Suzie was thrilled until she found out her new job required computer skills. She'd never touched a computer before, and quite frankly she was afraid of them.

When the time came for Suzie to do the computer training for her new job, she made up excuses to put it off and eventually called in sick. Her fear of technological change resulted in feelings of extreme stress and being overwhelmed. She couldn't fathom the amount of

9

C
A
S
E

S
T
U
D
Y

information she'd have to absorb. Ultimately, the "I can'ts" defeated her and sabotaged her one opportunity to keep a job.

Suzie's new supervisor should have seen through her smoke screen of excuses and probed deeper to find the truth. If this had happened, Suzie could have gotten the support she needed to develop her computer skills, starting with the basics. However, her fear and feelings of being stressed and overwhelmed kept her from asking for help.

Exercise: Seeing Through the Stress

After reading this section, answer the following questions:

1. What kinds of change have you experienced that have left you feeling stressed and overwhelmed?

   _____

   _____

   _____

2. How have these feelings altered your perceptions of reality?

   _____

   _____

   _____

3. What kinds of support or help would make you feel less stressed and overwhelmed?

   _____

   _____

   _____

4. What kinds of change have your co-workers experienced that have left them feeling stressed and overwhelmed?

   _____

   _____

   _____

9

5. How have these feelings altered their perceptions of reality?

_____

_____

_____

6. What kinds of support or help would make them feel less stressed and overwhelmed?

_____

_____

_____

Acting Out to Get Attention

Everyone needs and deserves attention in the workplace. If an employee can't get it from being positive and productive, then he'll get it by being Negative and nonproductive. This kind of behavior is self-sabotaging because the employee has either consciously or subconsciously acted in a way that keeps him from getting what he really wants.

If a good employee suddenly becomes tardy, excessively absent, shirks his responsibilities or falls off the mark in terms of work productivity or quality, this should be a red flag to the organization. Management needs to determine if Negative behavior is being reinforced more than positive behavior.

Case Study: Art's Antics

An excellent CPA, Art worked at the same accounting firm for 12 years preparing tax returns for the same clients. However, Art reached the point where he was bored with his job, and it began showing up in his quality of work and his relationships with co-workers. He began complaining about the firm, its policies, his workload and his boss. He was sarcastic to his fellow employees, and they, in turn, started complaining about him.

9

C A S E

S T U D Y

Art knew it was time for a job change, but both he and his boss avoided the issue. Secretly, Art longed to be a photographer — his lifelong hobby — but he didn't believe in himself enough to take the first step toward a career change.

Of course, Art's boss should have picked up on the Negative clues Art was dropping and addressed the situation before it got out of hand. Instead, his boss ignored the clues, thinking they were just temporary and would pass. He didn't want to lose a good, long-term employee like Art. Unfortunately, over time, things only got worse. The more the boss ignored Art, the more Art acted out his discontent. The only way to resolve this situation was for both of them to deal with it head-on.

Exercise: Figuring Out Acting It Out

After reading this section, answer the following questions:

1. In your workplace, do you receive attention for acting positively or Negatively?

   _____
   _____
   _____

2. What kinds of self-sabotaging behavior have you engaged in?

   _____
   _____
   _____

3. How could management help you resolve your situation?

   _____
   _____
   _____

C A S E S T U D Y

9

4. Do you know other employees who have received attention for acting Negatively rather than positively?

_____

_____

_____

5. What kinds of self-sabotaging behavior have they engaged in?

_____

_____

_____

6. How could you or their managers help them resolve their situation?

_____

_____

_____

9

Harboring Old Hurts and Resentments

Call it unfinished business. When an employee undergoes personal or professional setbacks, disappointments, disillusionments or traumas that are never resolved, she continues to carry these around with her. This excess baggage — as it's also known — travels with her from one work experience to the next. And everything that happens to her on the job is filtered through these old hurts and resentments. As a result, she's often perceived by others as having a chip on her shoulder or an "attitude" problem.

Case Study: Hortense's Old Hurts

Hortense has problems keeping a job. It all started when she got caught up in a messy divorce and was forced to sell the house she'd lived in for 10 years. She and her two teenagers moved into a cramped apartment. Then about six months later, she was laid off by the company for whom she'd worked since high-school graduation. Believe it not, things just went farther downhill from there.

C
A
S
E

S
T
U
D
Y

CASE STUDY

9

The only jobs Hortense seemed qualified for were demeaning and low paying. Each time she began a new job, she'd bring the old baggage along with her — the hurt, the resentment and the setbacks she'd faced since her divorce. And each time, she appeared timid, defensive, distant and short-tempered to her new co-workers and boss. Before long, she'd either quit that job or be fired because of her attitude. For Hortense, her past colored her future. She was caught in a never-ending Negative cycle that she couldn't escape.

Somewhere throughout her long list of jobs, at least one of Hortense's supervisors should have met with her to address her attitude and behavior. The supervisor could have started the conversation by asking these questions: "Are you happy here? Do you feel like you're appreciated? How are things working out for you?"

What Hortense needed was understanding and support. Instead, she'd hear things from her supervisors like: "You've got a bad temper and a bad attitude. You better shape up or you'll ship out!" A better supervisory response would have been "I've noticed that you sometimes get angry and defensive here at work. Is there a reason for that? Please realize we're only trying to do a good job not criticize you." A conversation like this would have softened any constructive criticism he had for Hortense and, at the same time, given her an opportunity to verbalize her hurt and resentment.

Exercise: Getting Past Old Hurts and Resentments

After reading this section, answer the following questions:

1. What unfinished business or excess baggage do you carry around with you?

    _____
    _____
    _____

2. How do these old hurts and resentments affect you in your current position?

_____

_____

_____

3. What kind of support and understanding might your manager provide to help you move beyond these old hurts and resentments?

_____

_____

_____

4. What unfinished business or excess baggage do your co-workers carry around with them?

_____

_____

_____

5. How do these old hurts and resentments affect them in their current positions?

_____

_____

_____

6. What kind of support and understanding might you provide to help them move beyond their old hurts and resentments?

_____

_____

_____

9

Questions for Personal Development

1. What is the major emphasis of this chapter?

   _____

   _____

   _____

2. What are the most important things you learned from this chapter?

   _____

   _____

   _____

3. How can you apply what you learned to your current job or your personal life?

   _____

   _____

   _____

4. How will you go about making these changes?

   _____

   _____

   _____

5. How can you monitor improvement?

   _____

   _____

   _____

6. Summarize the changes you expect to see in yourself and your co-workers one year from now.

   _____

   _____

   _____

9

C HAPTER 10

Overcoming Your Negaholism Once and For All

The moment of truth has arrived. You've taken The Negaholic Self-Assessment Tool found in Chapter One. You've learned about the four categories of Negaholics and met the Dirty Dozen. You've read countless case studies describing Negaholics.

Now ask yourself one last time: Do I recognize myself in any of these case studies? Do I ever exhibit Negaholic attitudes or behaviors? Am I a Negaholic? Be honest with your answers.

Negaholism's Seven-Step Program

People who want to overcome their addictions, such as alcoholics, often join support groups to help them. Many of these groups, like Alcoholics Anonymous, are based on a 12-step recovery program. For Negaholics, I've created a seven-step program.

Remember, admitting you're a Negaholic is the first step on the road to recovery. Here are seven others you can take to overcome your Negaholism once and for all.

1. Become aware of what you're doing.
2. Acknowledge what you do and what you want to change.
3. Choose to make the change.

4. Create a plan that builds a bridge between the present and your desired future.
5. Commit to the plan.
6. Follow up and follow through on your plan.
7. Set up external accountability.

Let's look at each one of these critical steps in more detail.

1. Become Aware of What You're Doing

If you're not aware of your actions and behaviors, then you can't possibly make any changes. Awareness comes from closely looking in the mirror and seeing yourself clearly ... perhaps for the first time.

Over the years, patterns of behavior become habitual and automatic, like shifting from first to second gear. They're easy to ignore or overlook. So the best way to become aware of them is to get feedback from an objective, trustworthy and supportive source, such as a family member, friend or co-worker. Then really listen to what they have to say.

2. Acknowledge What You Do and What You Want to Change

In this step, you tell yourself the truth. You admit that you're not perfect and that there's room for improvement, perhaps a complete overhaul. Then, you set goals for yourself. By doing this you've acknowledged your rundown condition and accepted the fact that change is needed.

3. Choose to Change

This is the most powerful of the seven steps. Making a choice like this is the essence of motivation. When you choose, you feel the "I cans" emerging and the beginning of self-motivation. It's at this point that you move from having a good idea or good intentions to putting yourself in the driver's seat. From there, you begin your trip down the road to recovery.

4. **Create a Plan That Builds a Bridge Between the Past and Your Desired Future**

   Your plan needs to be realistic, reasonable and attainable. Think of it as a series of short trips that will eventually lead you to a far-away yet reachable destination. Map out your trip and how you'll change from the person you are to the person you want to be. Remember that life is one long journey on the path toward continuous improvement. Never stop planning and never stop learning about yourself.

5. **Commit to the Plan**

   Without commitment, the best-laid plans go out the window. Commitment means that regardless of challenges and obstacles, you will find a way to achieve your goals and change. In fact, view each challenge or obstacle as an opportunity to prove your commitment.

   Although staying on course with your plan is very important, you'll inevitably encounter a few of these roadblocks and mishaps along the way. Just make the necessary adjustments and keep on driving toward your goals.

6. **Follow Up and Follow Through on Your Plan**

   Having follow-up checkpoints all along the route to your destination allows you to see how far you've come. (And you may be pleasantly surprised at how much progress you've actually made.) These checkpoints will help you stay focused on your goal and enhance your commitment to following through with your plan. They'll also help you keep track of all your accomplishments along the way.

7. **Set Up External Accountability**

   Don't set out on this journey all alone. Ask for guidance and support from someone you trust — from someone with whom you can share both your achievements and your setbacks. Whether he or she

> *"It is more important to know where you are going than to get there quickly. Do not mistake activity for achievement."*
>
> Mabel Newcomer

10

> *"Your friend is the man who knows all about you, and still likes you."*
>
> Elbert Hubbard

is a family member, friend, co-worker, boss, coach or mentor, this person must be someone with whom you can be totally honest and totally vulnerable.

Never be afraid to celebrate your accomplishments or admit your defeats in this person's company. Failure is only bad when you give up. Instead, recognize your mistakes, learn from them and recommit to your goals. Finally, be proud of what you are doing and where you are going.

When change challenges your choices and your competencies, you will need to reassess your goals, priorities and strategies. This quest for continuous improvement means that you reject complacency. As you progress and reach plateaus in your life, map out new destinations and new goals.

Exercise: Creating Your Own Seven-Step Plan

Think of a Negaholic attitude or behavior that you'd like to change in yourself, then answer the following questions:

1. Are you aware of what you're doing?

2. Have you acknowledged what you do and what you want to change?

3. Are you ready to choose to make the change?

4. What kind of plan will build a bridge between the present and your desired future?

_____

_____

_____

5. How will you commit to the plan?

_____

_____

_____

6. How will you follow up and follow through on your plan?

_____

_____

_____

7. How and with whom will you set up external accountability?

_____

_____

_____

Negaholic No More

Because Negaholism is a learned condition, it also can be unlearned and overcome. If you allow Negaholism to continue to hold you back, then you'll never achieve all that you, your team or your organization desires.

Overcoming Negaholism doesn't happen overnight. This process requires time, patience, desire, determination, commitment, a willingness to change, a belief in yourself and practicing all the tips and techniques outlined in this book. Once you begin to change, you'll be pleased with the positive results change brings to both your personal and professional lives. And it all starts with admitting you have a problem, identifying its source and working to overcome it.

"There are no shortcuts in evolution."

Louis D. Brandeis

Know what you want to achieve and be clear about your vision, mission and goals. Be willing to do whatever it takes to reach your desired outcome and destination. Remember, all things are possible if you believe in yourself, your team, your organization and your ability to bring about POSITIVE change.

Questions for Personal Development

1. What is the major emphasis of this chapter?

   _____

   _____

   _____

2. What are the most important things you learned from this chapter?

   _____

   _____

   _____

3. How can you apply what you learned to your current job or your personal life?

   _____

   _____

   _____

4. How will you go about making these changes?

   _____

   _____

   _____

5. How can you monitor improvement?

   _____

   _____

   _____

6. Summarize the changes you expect to see in yourself
   one year from now.

   _____

   _____

   _____

?

10

Index

A

B

10

P

R

S

T

V

W

10

Notes

Notes

Notes

Notes

YOUR BACK-OF-THE-BOOK STORE

Because you already know the value of National Press Publications Desktop Handbooks and Business User's Manuals, here's a time-saving way to purchase more career-building resources from our convenient "bookstore."

ORDER FORM

- IT'S EASY … Just make your selections, then visit us on the Web, mail, call or fax your order. (See back for details.)
- INCREASE YOUR EFFECTIVENESS … Books in these two series have sold more than two million copies and are known as reliable sources of instantly helpful information.
- THEY'RE CONVENIENT TO USE … Each handbook is durable, concise and filled with quality advice that will last you all the way to the boardroom.
- YOUR SATISFACTION IS 100% GUARANTEED. Forever.

60-MINUTE TRAINING SERIES™ HANDBOOKS

TITLE	RETAIL PRICE*	QTY.	TOTAL
8 Steps for Highly Effective Negotiations #424	$14.95		
Assertiveness #4422	$14.95		
Balancing Career and Family #4152	$14.95		
Common Ground #4122	$14.95		
The Essentials of Business Writing #4310	$14.95		
Everyday Parenting Solutions #4862	$14.95		
Exceptional Customer Service #4882	$14.95		
Fear & Anger: Control Your Emotions #4302	$14.95		
Fundamentals of Planning #4301	$14.95		
Getting Things Done #4112	$14.95		
How to Coach an Effective Team #4308	$14.95		
How to De-Junk Your Life #4306	$14.95		
How to Handle Conflict and Confrontation #4952	$14.95		
How to Manage Your Boss #493	$14.95		
How to Supervise People #4102	$14.95		
How to Work With People #4032	$14.95		
Inspire and Motivate: Performance Reviews #4232	$14.95		
Listen Up: Hear What's Really Being Said #4172	$14.95		
Motivation and Goal-Setting #4962	$14.95		
A New Attitude #4432	$14.95		
The New Dynamic Comm. Skills for Women #4309	$14.95		
The Polished Professional #4262	$14.95		
The Power of Innovative Thinking #428	$14.95		
The Power of Self-Managed Teams #4222	$14.95		
Powerful Communication Skills #4132	$14.95		
Present With Confidence #4612	$14.95		
The Secret to Developing Peak Performers #4962	$14.95		
Self-Esteem: The Power to Be Your Best #4642	$14.95		
Shortcuts to Organized Files and Records #4307	$14.95		
The Stress Management Handbook #4842	$14.95		
Supreme Teams: How to Make Teams Work #4303	$14.95		
Thriving on Change #4212	$14.95		
Women and Leadership #4632	$14.95		

MORE FROM OUR BACK-OF-THE-BOOK STORE
Business User's Manuals — Self-Study, Interactive Guide

TITLE	RETAIL PRICE	QTY.	TOTAL
The Assertive Advantage #439	$26.95		
Being OK Just Isn't Enough #5407	$26.95		
Business Letters for Busy People #449	$26.95		
Coping With Difficult People #465	$26.95		
Dealing With Conflict and Anger #5402	$26.95		
Hand-Picked: Finding & Hiring… #5405	$26.95		
High-Impact Presentation and Training Skills #4382	$26.95		
Learn to Listen #446	$26.95		
Lifeplanning #476	$26.95		
The Manager's Role as Coach #456	$26.95		
The Memory System #452	$26.95		
Negaholics® No More #5406	$26.95		
Parenting the Other Chick's Eggs #5404	$26.95		
Taking AIM On Leadership #5401	$26.95		
Prioritize, Organize: Art of Getting It Done 2nd ed. #4532	$26.95		
The Promotable Woman #450	$26.95		
Sex, Laws & Stereotypes #432	$26.95		
Think Like a Manager 3rd ed. #4513	$26.95		
Working Woman's Comm. Survival Guide #5172	$29.95		
In Canada $35.00			

<table>
<tr><td rowspan="4">SPECIAL OFFER:
Orders over $75 receive
<strong>FREE SHIPPING</strong></td><td><strong>Subtotal</strong></td><td>$</td></tr>
<tr><td>Add 7% Sales Tax
(Or add appropriate state and local tax)</td><td>$</td></tr>
<tr><td>Shipping and Handling
($3 one item; 50¢ each additional item)</em></td><td>$</td></tr>
<tr><td>Total</td><td>$</td></tr>
<tr><td></td><td colspan="2">VOLUME DISCOUNTS AVAILABLE — CALL 1-800-258-7248</td></tr>
</table>

Name_____Title_____

Organization _____

Address_____

City _____State/Province _____ZIP/Postal Code _____

Payment choices:
❏ Enclosed is my check/money order payable to National Seminars.
❏ Please charge to: ❏ MasterCard   ❏ VISA   ❏ American Express

Signature _____Exp. Date _____Card Number _____

❏ Purchase Order #_____

MAIL: Complete and mail order form   **PHONE:**   **FAX:**
      with payment to: Call toll-free **1-800-258-7248**   **1-913-432-0824**
      National Press Publications
      P.O. Box 419107   **INTERNET: www.natsem.com**
      Kansas City, MO 64141-6107